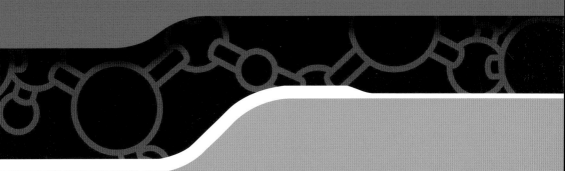

21st Century Science

The Earth

BROWN
BEAR
BOOKS

Published by Brown Bear Books Limited

An imprint of:
The Brown Reference Group Ltd
68 Topstone Road
Redding
Connecticut 06896
USA
www.brownreference.com

ISBN: 978-1-933834-75-7

Editorial Director: Lindsey Lowe
Managing Editor: Tim Harris
Project Director: Paul Humphrey
Editor: Rebecca Hunter
Designer: Barry Dwyer
Picture Researcher: Rebecca Hunter

Library of Congress Cataloging-in-Publication Data available upon request

Picture Credits

Cover Image
Desert (Shutterstock, Galyna AnDrushko)

Shutterstock:
7 Arvind Balaraman; 11 John Montgomery-Brown; 15 Jane McIlroy; 31 Gen Productions; 33 Vladislav Gurfinkel; 35 Jörg Jahn; 42 Brooke Whatnall; 46 Bjartur Snorrason; 52 Regien Paassen; 59 Mike Norton; 64 Korobanova; 71 Sam Dcruz; 74 George Burba; 79 Dr Flash; 81 Bychkov Kirill Alexandrovich; 83 Fernando Rodrigues; 89 Fred Goldstein; 94 Taiga; 98 Voyagerix; 99 left, Ppart; 99 right, Yoav Peled; 102 Wouter Tolenaars; 103 (from top) Vera Bogaerts, Paul Aniszewski, Pawel Kielpinski, Paul Banton; 105 Tphoto; 73 Johan Swanepoel; 81 Alejandro Mendoza R; 85 Kodda; 87 Otmar Smit

Artwork © The Brown Reference Group Ltd

The Brown Reference Group Ltd has made every effort to trace copyright holders of the pictures used in this book. Anyone having claims to ownership not identified above is invited to contact The Brown Reference Group Ltd.

Printed in the United States of America

Contents

Introduction	4–5	The Work of Rivers	62–64
Earth and Moon	6–7	Coasts and Oceans	65–67
Dynamic Planets	8–11	Deserts and Winds	68–70
Magma and Volcanoes	12–17	Glaciers and Ice	71–74
Seismic Waves	18–21	Life on Earth	75–77
Earth's Atmosphere	22–23	The Gaia Hypothesis	78–79
Earth's Oceans	24–26	Natural Catastrophes	80–82
The Early Continents	27–29	Global Climate	83–85
The Ice Ages	30–35	Recent Climate Change	86–89
Mobile and Stable Zones	36–39	Weather Patterns	90–92
Wandering Continents	40–42	Moving Oceans	93–95
Plates and Plumes	43–44	Seasonal Changes	96–98
Beneath the Ocean Floor	45–46	The World's Biomes	99–101
Island Arcs	47–49	On the Land	102–105
Mountains from the Sea	50–52	Glossary	106–107
Rift Valleys	53–54	Further Research	108–109
Geological Stories	55–57	Index	110–112
Nothing Is Forever	58–61		

Introduction

21st Century Science forms part of the Curriculum Connections project. Between them, the six volumes of this set cover all the key disciplines of the science curriculum: Chemistry, The Universe, Living Organisms, Genetics, The Earth, and Energy and Matter.

In-depth articles form the core of each volume, and focus on the scientific fundamentals. Each article relates to those preceding it, and the most basic are covered early in each volume. However, each article may be studied independently. So, for example, the Chemistry book begins with some relatively basic articles on atoms and molecules before progressing to more complex topics. However, the student who already has a reasonable background knowledge can turn straight to the article about carbon-hydrogen compounds to gain a more thorough understanding.

Within each article there are two key aids to learning that are to be found in color bars located in the margins of each page:

Curriculum Context sidebars indicate to the reader that a subject has particular relevance to certain key State and National Science and Technology Education Standards up to Grade 12.

Glossary sidebars define key words within the text.

A summary Glossary lists the key terms defined in the volume, and the Index lists people and major topics covered.

Fully captioned illustrations play a major role in the set, including photographs, artwork reconstructions, and explanatory diagrams.

About this Volume

Our planet is part of a system of worlds that comprise the Sun's family, including the other planets, comets, meteoroids, and asteroids. All were created, together with the Sun itself, about 4.6 billion years ago out of a cloud of gases.

The scientific study of Earth—geology—began in Europe in the 17th and 18th centuries, and since about the same dates scientists have also been able to study the Moon and the planets through telescopes. Our understanding of the structure and composition of Earth has undergone vast changes since the beginning of the 1960s, when the concept of plate tectonics was proposed to explain continental drift, the distribution of regions vulnerable to earthquakes and volcanoes, and other phenomena. This theory has given geologists new insights into how the rigid outer surfaces of some planets adjust to the internal movements of their mantles and cores. Scientists have learned how Earth's crust is continually being generated and destroyed at certain sites, where huge slabs of the lithosphere jostle against one another.

By understanding better the forces at work within Earth, geologists have been able to make more meaningful comparisons with the other planets. It seems that no other planet has such a dynamic structure as Earth's.

Also investigated in this volume are environmental problems—including the destruction of natural systems, overuse of resources, pollution, chlorofluorocarbons, and global warming—and their impacts on humanity. Ecology seeks solutions to these urgent problems by understanding their full context: exactly how human demands on Earth affect its natural systems and how these systems interrelate with each other and with all the species they support.

Earth and Moon

Energy from the Sun bathes its attendant family of planets, which travel in almost circular orbits around it. The planets shine in the reflecting sunlight; they do not generate light by nuclear reactions. Earth is one of an inner group of four rocky planets, including Mercury, Venus, and Mars. Farther out are four much larger bodies, two of which (Jupiter and Saturn) are composed primarily of gas, and two predominantly of ice (Uranus and Neptune).

Curriculum Context

Students should know how the differences and similarities among the Sun, the terrestrial planets, and the gas planets may have been established during the formation of the Solar System.

Moon

A natural satellite of a major planetary body. The moons of the Solar System range from huge bodies the size of Earth's Moon to tiny chunks of rock known as shepherd moons that rotate within Saturn's ring system.

Small rocky asteroids are concentrated in orbits between those of Mars and Jupiter. Many such objects crashed into the solid surfaces of the planets during the early years of the Solar System, forming impact craters and large basins. The Sun's family is completed by icy comets which originated in the far reaches of the Solar System and have mainly parabolic orbits. Many come close to the Earth and become spectacular objects in the night sky. Meteors are other small objects that often enter the Earth's atmosphere.

Many of the planets have rock and ice moons, or orbiting systems of rings. Although not the largest of the natural satellites, the Earth's Moon is a splendid object and was the first extraterrestrial world to be visited by astronauts, in 1969.

Gravity and tides

The Moon is unusually large in relation to its planetary neighbor, with a diameter more than a quarter that of the Earth. The two are often seen as a double planet system, orbiting around a common point deep within the Earth. The strong gravitational pull of the Moon upon the Earth, and its oceans in particular, gives rise to twice-daily tides.

Monthly orbit

The Moon orbits the Earth at a mean distance of 238,323 miles (384,392 kilometers). It takes one month to complete each revolution and the same period to rotate once on its axis. As a result it directs the same face toward the Earth at all times, and the far side is never seen from Earth. The Moon's monthly phases are dependent on the angle between the Earth, Sun, and Moon at different times. There are also occasionally lunar eclipses, when the Earth casts its shadow on the Moon.

The Moon is a natural satellite of the Earth and is the fifth largest satellite in the Solar System.

At one time it was believed that the Moon derived from the Earth, somehow ejected from the Pacific, but this idea is now discounted. Modern research suggests that soon after the Earth's core had formed, a massive celestial object gave the Earth a glancing blow. This object was vaporized, and the Moon formed largely from its mantle. This explains why the Moon and Earth are chemically dissimilar and why the Moon lost all of its volatile constituents.

The mean density of the Moon is significantly less than that of the Earth. Since much of the Earth's high average density derives from the heavy material in its core, this suggests that, unlike Earth, the Moon does not have a large, dense core.

Dynamic Planets

The Earth is a truly dynamic world, to which active volcanism, tectonism, and atmospheric phenomena bear witness. The outer gas and ice giant planets, with their short rotation periods and large masses, have also maintained vigorous atmospheric circulation and sufficiently active core motions to generate magnetic fields. Yet some planets, although active during the earlier stages of the Solar System's history, have become inert. Others experience only modest geological or atmospheric activity.

Curriculum Context

Students should know the evidence from geological studies of Earth and other planets suggest that the early Earth was very different from Earth today.

Isotope

One of a number of forms of an element that has the same number of protons in the nucleus but a different tally of neutrons (and therefore a different relative atomic mass).

The differences in the degree of dynamism of the inner planets is a reflection of their mass and distance from the Sun. Planets with small mass accumulated modest amounts of accretional energy and lost this relatively quickly. Small bodies such as the Moon "froze" geologically during the first billion years or so of geological time. Mercury, being so close to the Sun, has been stripped of any atmosphere it did have.

More massive worlds, such as Venus, Earth, and Mars, originally gained more energy from accretion and subsequently from decay of long-lived radioactive isotopes. They maintained relatively high levels of geological or atmospheric activity for much longer—for Venus and Earth, up to the present. On smaller Mars, geological activity is now the result of winds, glaciation, and atmospheric processes.

The first crusts

At a relatively early stage, all of the inner planets developed solid crusts made from silicate rocks. These were gradually built up as material from the planetary mantles beneath was extruded to form basaltic lavas. The Earth's primordial crust has long since been returned to the mantle. But clues as to its likely appearance are forthcoming from our nearest neighbor, the Moon, which (because its geological activity terminated over 2 billion years ago) retains most of its ancient features.

The Moon's ancient highland crust is made up of an igneous rock called anorthosite, which is composed in large part of the aluminum silicate mineral plagioclase feldspar. It is chemically enriched in lithophile elements, which have high melting points. This rather thick crust appears to have crystallized around 4.4 billion years ago from an "ocean" of magma rich in aluminum, calcium, and silica.

Curriculum Context

Students should know the evidence from Earth and Moon rocks indicates that the Solar System was formed from a nebular cloud of dust and gas approximately 4.6 billion years ago.

The Life of the Moon

In the early stages of its history—between 4.5 and 4.0 billion years ago—the Moon, like the four inner planets, underwent catastrophic bombardment by meteorites and asteroids, destroying most of the recently formed crust. Huge impact craters and basins were left as scars on the surface.

From about 3.9 billion to 3.0 billion years ago, magma from the still-molten core of the Moon rose to the surface through volcanic activity, filling many of its basins and forming maria— dark plains, or "seas," of lava, whose edges form chains of lunar mountains. The stages of this process created layers of maria—mirroring stratification of layers of rock on Earth.

After an intervening period of minor volcanic activity and cratering, the Moon's surface has changed very little in the past 1 billion years.

The Moon bears the scars of an intense bombardment by meteoroids and asteroids which continued up to about 4.0 billion years ago. This left the imprint of huge impact basins and myriad impact craters, ranging in size from tiny microcraters measuring only a few microns across to great ring structures several hundreds of miles in diameter. The final size of the craters, however, is less than the cavity which was created on impact, as it was modified by decompression after the event.

Associated with the craters and basins are extensive blankets of material thrown out in response to the cratering process. These now form a complex and extensive succession of interleaving layers on top of the crustal base. The highly shattered surface layer is called the regolith. On Earth, this has become soil.

The Earth's crust

The composition of the Earth's early crust must have differed from that of the Moon. It was probably richer in iron and magnesium and had a lower percentage of high-temperature silicates. It was built up by the repeated outflow of highly fluid magmas often found in connection with volcanoes. Soon after it began to crystallize, the crust was thin, and magmas easily pierced the fragile skin. In time, as layer upon layer accumulated, it became more difficult for this to happen and eruptions became focused where the crust was thinner or weaker.

This crust suffered the same intense bombardment as did the Moon, despite the shielding effect of the Earth's early atmosphere. Like those of the Moon, the rocks were intensely shattered and contained high-pressure forms of silicate minerals such as coesite. Subsequently this early crust was "recycled" due to plate tectonic activity, which moves the ocean floor and the continents with it, pushing down surface layers of crust

Curriculum Context

Students should know that features of the ocean floor (magnetic patterns, age, and sea-floor topography) provide evidence of plate tectonics.

Plate tectonics

The theory of the Earth that invokes the movement of lithospheric plates as an explanation of processes such as volcanism, seismicity, and orogenesis.

and allowing new material to be pushed up. This process is still occurring on Earth. Because the material is recycled, the size of the lithosphere remains constant; it neither expands nor contracts.

Inner planets' crusts

The primeval crusts of the other inner planets must have been similar to those of Earth, but unlike Earth's, each retains an extensive record of impact. On Mercury, Venus, and Mars, the most ancient cratered regions are partly obliterated by younger volcanic plains (intercrater plains), which indicate that extensive volcanism continued after the main phase of cratering had ended. The number of small impact craters on the Venusian crust is significantly less than on Mercury or the Moon. This is because the planet's dense atmosphere had a shielding effect, winnowing out smaller meteoroids as they entered it.

The crusts of Earth and Venus have never become sufficiently thick to prevent magma reaching the surface from inside. However, the smaller planets eventually reached a point where the thickening of their crusts prevented further volcanism. At this stage, modification of the surface by processes from within the planet effectively ceased. The Moon and Mercury are considered geologically dead.

Fast-moving lava from a volcano cools in the air and solidifies, forming ropy strands called pahoehoe. Planetary crusts were thickened by frequent extrusions of such fluid lava—a process that continues to occur on Earth, although it happens mostly at fissures in the crust underwater, rather than by the more obvious eruptions above ground.

Magma and Volcanoes

The temperature inside the Earth near the surface rises, on average, 5°F (3°C) with each 330 feet (100 meters) in depth; about 30 miles (50 kilometers) below the surface, it is about 1,830°F (1,000°C). The gradient decreases at greater depths, and the core probably does not exceed 7,770°F (4,300°C).

Despite these temperatures there is only a narrow zone within the upper mantle, known as the asthenosphere (43 to 155 miles, or 70 to 250 kilometers below the surface), where molten rock or magma is found. Below this is a solid region of the mantle, the mesosphere, where enormous pressure prevents the rock from melting. The iron-rich outer core is also molten, at between 6700° and 7770°F (3700° and 4300°C) , but the high pressures in the inner core make that solid too.

Molten rock may be forced up to the surface as lava. It may flow quietly or explode to form an eruption cloud. Whether the lava is explosive depends on how deep it formed, what sort of volcano is involved, how viscous the magma is, what volatile elements it contains, and so on.

Magma

Most types of magma are silicates and give rise to igneous rocks built from minerals with the silica molecule (SiO_2) in them. As they rise toward the surface, they expand and cool, and eventually begin to crystallize. In addition to silica, terrestrial magmas contain elements such as aluminum, iron, magnesium, calcium, titanium, manganese, phosphorus, sodium, and potassium. These combine with the silica to form silicates. Silica accounts for between 35 and 75 percent of terrestrial magmas. Those with low silica content are basic, while those with a high silica content are called

Curriculum Context

Students must be able to describe and differentiate the layers of Earth and the interactions among them.

Magma

Molten rock or other mineral material, usually of silicate composition, that is formed in the lower crust or mantle of the Earth. When it solidifies, it is known as igneous rock; when it emerges through the crust it is known as lava.

acidic or silicic. Also present in smaller amounts are trace elements such as rubidium, strontium, zinc, sulfur, and cobalt. Finally, there are many volatile substances. The most important of these is water, accompanied by elements such as boron, chlorine , fluorine, and compounds containing sulfur, hydrogen, oxygen, and nitrogen.

Under pressure

While the magma is pressurized deep inside the Earth, these elements and compounds are dissolved within it.

Temperatures inside the Earth

The temperature rises very quickly in the first 620 miles (1000 km) below the Earth's surface, but the temperature rise flattens out at the boundary between the outer and inner cores, about 3100 miles (5000 km) below the surface.

Scientists have estimated these temperatures by studies of the melting points of mantle material and iron at pressures equivalent to those thought to prevail at various depths. Seismic surveys have indicated the zones where melting is found. These are associated with temperatures that give rise to phase changes (solid to liquid, or liquid to solid).

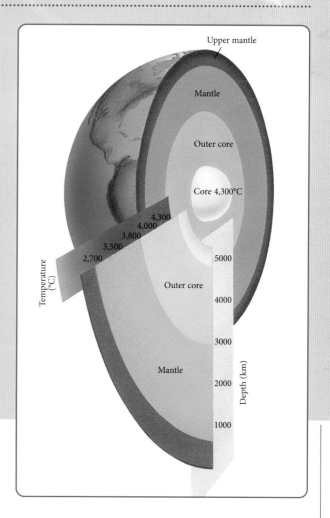

As the magma rises and the pressure drops, the more volatile components expand and are released as gases. Thus, when a melt reaches the surface, it consists of a mixture of crystals, liquid, and gases. Indeed, the expansion of the gas component is in large part responsible for forcing the magma to the surface, and possibly causing an explosive eruption.

Even at the enormous temperatures and pressures found in the asthenosphere where the magmas form, the "dry" mantle material cannot actually melt. Volatile elements, however, can lower the melting point of silicate minerals by as much as 930°F (500°C), and water in this region of the mantle allows melting to occur. This process is called partial melting.

As the mostly solid mantle convects, hot material rises and cool material falls. Semimolten material in the asthenosphere is less dense than the lithosphere on top of it. The hot, less dense material collects in localized bulges (Rayleigh Taylor instabilities) and forms diapirs or "plumes" that become sources of magma.

Mantle upwelling
Continental crust
70 km
Asthenosphere
250 km
Solid mantle

Water cycling

Studies of silicates such as amphiboles and micas, which are sometimes brought up as blocks within magmas from the mantle, indicate that they contain significant amounts of water. More water reaches the mantle as the Earth's crust, including water-laden sediments, is recycled and returned to the mantle through tectonic processes.

Curriculum Context

Students should know how to explain the properties of rocks based on the physical and chemical conditions in which they formed.

Fractional crystallization

Partial melts are less dense than the surrounding mantle and tend to rise as bulbous bodies called diapirs. When crystallization begins inside the diapir, the first crystals that form are more dense than the surrounding liquid, and tend to sink within it. If the deeper, crystal-laden part of a diapir is tapped, the melt that rises has a different composition from the largely liquid upper region. This process, called fractional crystallization, explains how different types of magma can arise from the same region of mantle.

Vast volumes of fluid basalt lavas were extruded in the northwest British Isles between 65 and 50 million years ago—most extruded from fissures in the Earth's crust. Such lavas occur in the first stages of continental rifting at divergent plate margins. The beautiful hexagonal joints as seen here at the Giant's Causeway, County Antrim, Northern Ireland, formed as the lava cooled and contracted.

Volcanoes

Volcanic regions are concentrated along the boundaries of tectonic plates—vast blocks of moving crust. Where plates diverge, as in mid-ocean, magma and gas escape unnoticed from rifts in the sea floor rocks and generate new oceanic crust out of basaltic rocks. Where sub-oceanic ridges rise above sea level, volcanoes may produce new islands.

Oceanic basalt is low in silica, which means it tends to be fluid and can escape easily. A quite different magma is found in regions where two tectonic plates collide and one dives below the other, such as along the western border of the Pacific. Here, the typical magmas are more siliceous, gas-rich, and viscous, and their escape is marked by violent explosive activity, as at Mount St. Helens (in the United States) and Mount Pinatubo (in the Philippines). These volcanoes have the classic cone shape. They are built from lavas and pyroclastic rocks, which are composed of particles blasted out from vents. Dangerous ground-hugging mixtures of gas, lava, and pyroclastic materials may sweep down the flanks of the volcanoes, burying or asphyxiating anything in their path. These *nuées ardentes* ("glowing avalanches") are often deadly, as are lahars (mudflows), which are triggered by storms and torrential rains after eruptions, particularly in tropical regions.

Hot spots

Some of the largest but least dangerous volcanoes on Earth sit above what are called hot spots—uprising "plumes" of hotter-than-average mantle material. Such massive lava shields have gently sloping profiles which, in the Hawaiian Islands, rise as much as 6 miles (10 km) above the ocean floor, and have diameters of more than 62 miles (100 km).

A volcano cone is built up of layers of lava (extruded magma) and pyroclastic material (fine dust, ash, and blocks) cut by sills, dikes, and plugs. Eruptions occur through a central vent and side vents. The blast leaves a depression that may become filled with a lake, or remain as a caldera more than half a mile (1 km) in diameter.

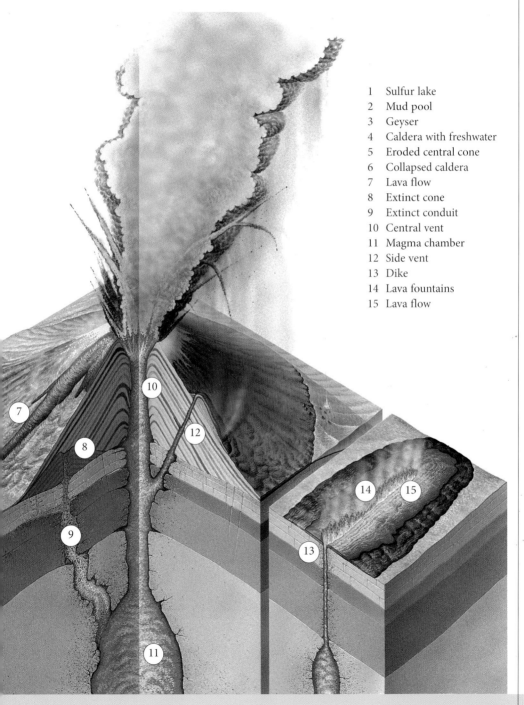

1   Sulfur lake
2   Mud pool
3   Geyser
4   Caldera with freshwater
5   Eroded central cone
6   Collapsed caldera
7   Lava flow
8   Extinct cone
9   Extinct conduit
10 Central vent
11 Magma chamber
12 Side vent
13 Dike
14 Lava fountains
15 Lava flow

Seismic Waves

Dynamic planets are marked by their internal activity, which is expressed at their surfaces in volcanoes and the tectonic movement of plates, and in earthquakes. This activity is significant in other ways: the passage of seismic waves through the interior enables geophysicists to probe parts of the Earth that are otherwise inaccessible. By doing so they have been able to demonstrate that our planet has a layered structure. This is true also of the other inner planets, and simple seismic studies have been made of both the Moon and Mars.

Seismometer

A sensitive instrument for recording seismic waves. The original instruments used a very sensitive spring to record vibrations caused by seismic events.

Each time rising magma displaces the rocks of the crust, or each time brittle rocks fail, sound or "seismic" tremors are set off. They are propagated through the Earth with velocities proportional to the density of the medium through which they travel. They can be recorded on delicate instruments called seismographs, and chains of these have been set up throughout the world to record the quakes that occur daily.

The Richter Scale

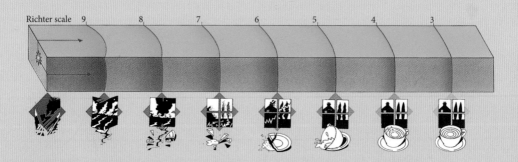

The Richter scale expresses the intensity of seismic events by measuring the frequency and amplitude of their surface waves. The scale, from 0 to 10, is logarithmic: increases of 1 along the scale represents an increase of a factor of 10 in intensity, so that magnitude 5 is 100 times stronger than magnitude 3. Severe earthquakes are greater than 7.

Not all seismic waves are the same. P waves (primary or pressure waves) are compressional in type and move with a "push-pull" motion through solids, liquids, and gases. Each molecular disturbance they effect displaces atoms over distances of around 30–40 feet (10–13 meters). In contrast, S waves have a shearing motion and travel at about 60 percent of the velocity of P waves. They can be transmitted only through solids.

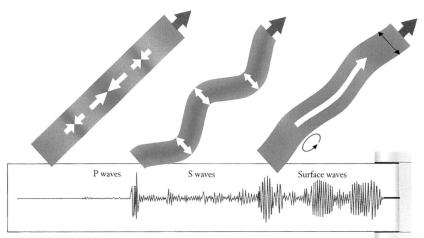

P (primary or pressure) waves have a push–pull motion and displace the atoms in solids and liquids. They travel faster than S waves and arrive first at a seismic recording station.

S (secondary or shear) waves are produced by shear deformation that occurs perpendicular to the direction of travel. They travel at about 60 percent of the velocity of P Waves.

Both P and S waves (surface waves) may reach the surface of the Earth and travel along it. Unlike seismic shocks, nuclear explosions do not produce surface waves.

When an earthquake occurs, seismic waves are sent out from the focus; the point on the surface immediately above this is termed the epicenter. The intensity of the quake is measured on the Richter scale; the largest have a magnitude of about 9. The position of the epicenter from a seismograph station is obtained by measuring the difference in arrival times of P and S waves. Records from at least three stations are needed to do this.

Curriculum Context

Students should know why and how earthquakes occur and the scales used to measure their intensity and magnitude.

Seismic Wave Movement

Seismic waves travel through the Earth and can be detected by seismometers. The waves do not travel in straight lines but are refracted by changes in the interior layers of the Earth. A "shadow zone" occurs where no waves reach the surface.

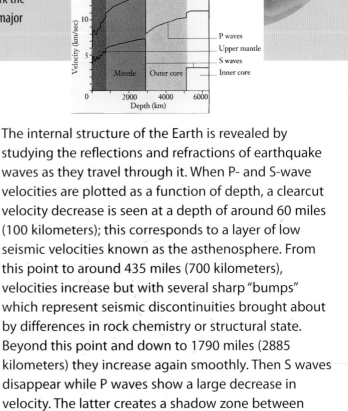

Seismic waves travel faster with depth. At certain depths, sudden changes in their velocity give rise to seismic discontinuities, which mark the boundaries between the major layers of the Earth.

The internal structure of the Earth is revealed by studying the reflections and refractions of earthquake waves as they travel through it. When P- and S-wave velocities are plotted as a function of depth, a clearcut velocity decrease is seen at a depth of around 60 miles (100 kilometers); this corresponds to a layer of low seismic velocities known as the asthenosphere. From this point to around 435 miles (700 kilometers), velocities increase but with several sharp "bumps" which represent seismic discontinuities brought about by differences in rock chemistry or structural state. Beyond this point and down to 1790 miles (2885 kilometers) they increase again smoothly. Then S waves disappear while P waves show a large decrease in velocity. The latter creates a shadow zone between 103° and 143° from an earthquake focus. This marks the boundary between the mantle and the outer core, and is sometimes known as the Gutenberg discontinuity, after its discovery in 1909 by the German–American geologist Beno Gutenberg. The S-wave behavior indicates that the outer core itself is liquid.

The Mohorovicic discontinuity

The Mohorovicic discontinuity (Moho for short) lies where the velocity of P waves changes abruptly. It is found about 4 miles (7 kilometers) below the oceanic crust, and as much as 25–43 miles (40–70 kilometers)

P and S waves radiate away in many different directions from an earthquake focus. The waves are refracted as they pass though materials of different densities. Because they are deflected by the Earth's core, P waves do not reach the surface at certain points, giving rise to a "shadow zone."

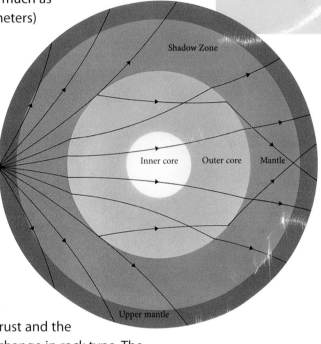

below the surface of the continents. It defines the boundary between the crust and the mantle, where there is a change in rock type. The dominant rock type below the Moho is peridotite; above it, the oceanic crust is mainly basaltic, whereas the continental crust is closer in composition to granite. Two further seismic discontinuities occur within the mantle, at depths of 248 and 415 miles (400 and 670 kilometers). They correspond to phase changes brought about by increasing pressure which has a severe effect upon the structures of the minerals that occur there. The core itself is believed to have the same composition as iron meteorites.

Curriculum Context

The student is expected to analyze the processes that power the movement of the Earth's continental and oceanic plates and identify the effects of this movement, including faulting, folding, earthquakes, and volcanic activity.

Earth's Atmosphere

The gaseous envelope surrounding a planet forms its atmosphere. Earth's earliest atmosphere consisted of gases that escaped from the planet's interior. In decreasing order of abundance, these would have been methane, water, ammonia, and hydrogen sulfide. The water molecules were split by the Sun's energy into hydrogen (which escaped to space), and oxygen, which oxidized methane to carbon dioxide.

Atmosphere

The layer of gases that surround a planetary object. Earth's atmosphere is divisible into a number of layers with different temperatures and pressures. The weather is confined to the lowest layer, the troposphere.

Carbon dioxide began to react with silicates, forming carbonates, and was removed from the air. If this atmospheric carbon had not thus been fixed, the evolution of the Earth's atmosphere might have taken a very different course.

When, about 3.5 billion years ago, bacteria evolved on Earth, they began to exploit the energy contained in carbon dioxide through photosynthesis, giving off free oxygen as a by-product. This began the process of releasing the Earth's oxygen that had been bound up in compounds.

Today, nitrogen accounts for about 80 percent by volume of the air, with oxygen making up most of the remainder. Although water vapor, carbon dioxide, and ozone are present in much smaller amounts, they are vitally important, because they have the ability to absorb infrared radiation and thus affect atmospheric and surface temperature. Overall, the chemical composition of the atmosphere is remarkably uniform.

Clouds play a role in maintaining the delicate balance between solar (incoming) and thermal (outgoing) radiation levels. At any one time, approximately half of the Earth's surface is covered by cloud.

Layers of atmosphere

The Earth's atmosphere occurs in four main layers, which are caused by variations in temperature and pressure resulting from the distribution of solar heating. These are three levels near ground level at which temperatures are highest: one near the surface in the troposphere, where visible and infrared radiation is absorbed; one about 30 miles (50 kilometers) above the surface, in the stratosphere, where ozone absorbs ultraviolet radiation; and the third several hundred miles up, in the thermosphere, where ultraviolet is absorbed by photoionization processes.

Clouds and weather systems on Earth are the result of interactions between the atmosphere and the oceans. Winds are responsible for moving these systems over large distances, sometimes extremely vigorously. Most weather occurs in the troposphere (up to 7 miles or 11 kilometers) above the surface). The boundary between this and the stratosphere is known as the tropopause.

Curriculum Context

Students should know how differential heating of the Earth results in circulation patterns in the atmosphere and oceans that globally distribute the heat.

Other Planets' Atmospheres

The atmospheres of the outer planets are in large part composed of hydrogen compounds, and they rotate rapidly. The relatively small difference in temperature between equator and poles means that heat transfer processes are rather different from those of Earth. Unlike the other giants, Jupiter has an internal source of heat, and does not have to rely on the rather weak solar radiation to supply it with thermal energy. The thick atmosphere of Uranus is mainly hydrogen, helium, and methane.

| Venus | Earth | Mars | Jupiter | Saturn |

Earth's Oceans

Low-lying and filled with water, the oceans are geologically distinct from the continents on Earth, and their characteristics are the result of tectonic plate movements. Under the oceans are extensive linear submarine ridges and deep trenches, separated by flat abyssal plains. Oceanic crust forms at divergent plate margins and is destroyed along convergence zones. The plates are "recycled" quickly enough to ensure that no oceanic crust forming the floor of a modern ocean is more than 200 million years old.

Gabbro

A coarse-grained igneous rock which is chemically equivalent to basalt. Essential minerals found in gabbro are the calcium-rich plagioclase feldspar and pyroxene, usually the variety augite.

Curriculum Context

Students should be able to describe the geological development of the present-day oceans and identify commonly found features.

The crust itself has a mean density of around 1.8 ounces pounds per cubic inch (3.1 grams per cubic centimeter) and is veneered with sediments. The upper 1.5 miles (2.5 kilometers) is composed of basaltic rocks. These are underlain by coarser gabbro rocks, which are 3 miles (5 kilometers) thick. Beneath this is a thin layer of even denser rocks, then the mantle itself.

Marine sedimentary rocks more than 3.5 billion years old prove that oceans are at least as ancient as the first continents. At that date there must already have been water-filled basins in the outer skin of the Earth. The water originated from the gases and vapors released by volcanoes. Today the oceans cover more than two-thirds of the Earth's surface area; in the past the percentage was greater because the early continents were smaller.

Sea salt

Seawater contains a wide range of chemical elements—primarily chloride, sulfate, sodium, and magnesium, with calcium and potassium next in importance. Its salinity (33 to 38 parts per thousand) is remarkably constant over enormous areas and only differs near ice-sheets. It represents a standard solution with varying dilutions. The salts derive from the weathering of continental rocks and are transported to the oceans by rivers. The early oceans were probably less saline than today's, because the smaller continents that existed in the past would have supplied the oceans with less salt.

Another source of salt for the oceans are hydrothermal springs, which were only recently discovered on submarine ridges by the submersible research vessel *Alvin*. At such places, water passing through newly formed crust carries virtually all of the salts of iron, manganese, lithium, and barium found in sea water. Furthermore, large quantities of silica and calcium originate here, as well as carbon dioxide.

Carbon dioxide

The carbon dioxide content of oceans depends on an interchange of ocean water with the atmosphere. Thus,

Oceanic ridges

A global network of ridges crosses the floors of the oceans. They rise many thousands of feet above the abyssal plain, have a linear form, and crests that are dissected by rifting.

Underwater Mountains

Underneath the oceans' waters lie the most imposing physical structures on Earth. Huge mountains (ridges) of basalt—up to 2½ miles (4 km) high, 250 miles (400 km) wide, and 25,000 miles (40,000 km) long—divide the oceans into sections.

Two of the most important ridges are the Mid-Atlantic Ridge and the East Pacific Rise. On the ocean floor, trenches hundreds of miles long run parallel to the edges of continents and extend to depths lower than 4 miles (7 km).

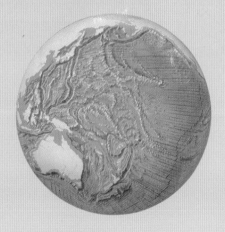

if carbon dioxide is added to the air, roughly one half of it enters the sea. Once in seawater, it exists in equilibrium with carbonic acid (H_2CO_3) and carbonate ions. In water of depths up to around 3 miles (5 kilometers), carbonate tends to be precipitated; below this level it does not. This allows organisms to utilize it in the shallower waters to form their shells, without danger of depletion.

Oceanic currents

Oceanic circulation is driven by differences in the density of seawater, due to differing salinity and temperature. In general, the lower the temperature the greater the density; however, water reaches its maximum density at 39.2°F (4°C). Down to depths of between 330 to 650 feet (100 to 200 meters) the surface waters are heated by the Sun and stirred by winds and waves. Below this depth, or thermocline, there is a sharp fall in temperature; 35–39°F (2–4°C) is typical.

The dominant factors in the present circulation pattern of Earth's oceans are the temperature and salinity differences created in the southern oceans by alternate freezing and thawing of Antarctic ice. In the past, the pattern of land and sea was different. For instance, when the supercontinent known as Pangea split in two during the Mesozoic era, an equatorial seaway opened around the world, allowing warm water to spread in both north and south latitudes.

Curriculum Context

Students should know the relationship between the rotation of Earth and the circular motions of ocean currents and air in pressure centers.

Satellites in orbit around the Earth and other scientific investigations have revealed the global circulation of the ocean water. This global conveyor, as it is commonly called, functions as our planet's gigantic central-heating system.

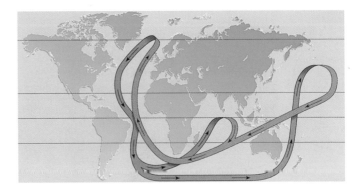

The Early Continents

Earth's continents today cover about 30 percent of its surface. Made from rocks of lower density than the ocean floor, they "float" above the heavier rocks of the mantle. Continental crust varies between 12 and 55 miles (20 and 90 kilometers) thick, being greatest beneath major mountain ranges. The oldest reliably dated continental massifs are 3.9 billion years old. The structure of continental regions is much more complex than that of the younger oceans. Continents are oldest in their centers and younger toward their margins.

Cratons, or shields, are found at the heart of most continents. They are composed of deformed metamorphic rocks intruded by granite rocks. Cratons are the remnants of ancient mountain chains. They are surrounded by stable platforms where a thick layer of horizontal sedimentary rocks has accumulated on top of cratonic rocks. Adjacent to stable platforms are younger orogenic or mountain-building belts: linear zones of compressed fold mountains produced by the collision between two continental plates, or between a continental and an ocean plate, as in the Andes mountains in South America.

The continents grew in stages rather than all at once. About 10 percent of the continental crust was produced in the Archean between 3.8 and 3.5 billion years ago; a further 60 percent also between 2.9 and 2.6 billion years ago; and the remaining 30 percent during major continent-building phases in the later Proterozoic era (1.9 through 1.7 and 1.19 through 0.9 billion years ago) and the Phanerozoic, which began around 590 million years ago.

No one is sure how the first continental crust formed. Geochemical research suggests that partial melting of oceanic crust produced a "primordial crust," which

Craton

A region of ancient crust at the heart of a continent, which has evaded tectonic deformation for a protracted period.

Curriculum Context

Students should know how to explain the properties of rocks based on the physical and chemical conditions in which they formed, including plate tectonic processes.

differed from oceanic material. This was reworked continually by vigorous convective motions within the mantle and by meteorites. Early continents resulting from this process were small.

Subduction zones

Another explanation for the development of the continents involves subduction zones within the oceanic crust. Where two oceanic plates collide, one is driven beneath the other, causing the crustal rocks to melt and volcanoes to result. New rocks are generated, forming an island arc. Such structures, built from rock slightly less dense than the ocean floor, might have formed early continental cores, but there is no proof that they formed the first continental blocks.

More recently, continent growth was the result of plate movements. The most important of these is sea-floor

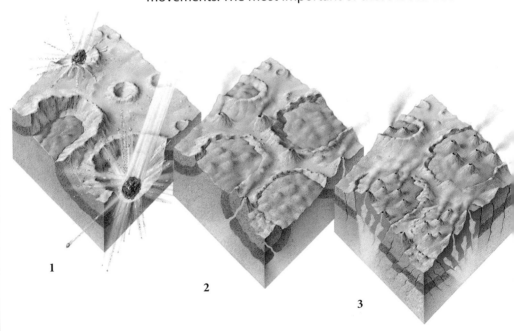

1   2   3

One theory of original continental growth begins with meteorites crashing into the newly-formed Earth (1), piercing the crust and causing magma to flow out (2). Igneous rock that formed in this region differed from that around it (3).

spreading, which causes the continents to change shape and position. Things may have been different in Archean times when the crust was thinner, the Earth's interior hotter and mantle convection very vigorous. It seems likely that continents were then smaller and more numerous, while the plates were thinner and more readily deformable.

Curriculum Context

The student is expected to analyze methods of tracking continental and oceanic plate movement.

Continental and Oceanic Crusts

Continental crust is much thicker and more varied in its composition than oceanic crust. In the crust directly below the Andes, for example, is a huge section of sedimentary and volcanic rock; the same section beneath Wisconsin is tiny, and is smaller yet in the oceanic crust. These layers are estimated from changes in seismic velocities at different depths (called seismic discontinuities).

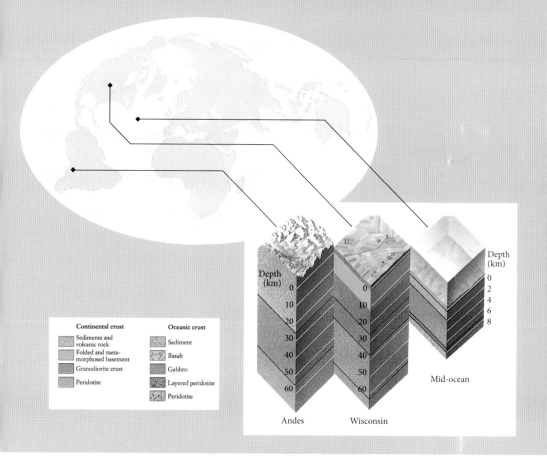

Continental crust	Oceanic crust
Sediments and volcanic rock	Sediment
Folded and meta-morphosed basement	Basalt
Granodiorite crust	Gabbro
Peridotite	Layered peridotite
	Peridotite

The Ice Ages

At various times during its history, the Earth has been subject to glaciations, when vast layers of ice spread from the poles over the land and oceans. Such events have left their marks in the rocks of every continent and have given vital clues to geologists trying to understand the Earth's history.

During the Permo-Carboniferous glaciation, the continents were in very different positions from today. This was shown by the discovery of glacial remains over Africa up to the Equator, southern India, the southern portion of Australia, and the eastern regions of south America. All were then near the South Pole, and part of Pangea.

During a glacial period, it is not continuously cold, and the cold spells are punctuated by interglacials during which temperatures are far higher. Today we are living in an interglacial, toward the close of the Pleistocene ice age: this began some 10 million years ago and its ice sheets retreated to their present position about 10,000 years ago.

Early Ice Ages

The earliest known glacial deposits are found near Lake Huron in Canada. Three layers of glacial deposits, dated between 2.7 and 1.8 billion years old, cover an area of 46,000 square miles (120,000 square kilometers). The glacial sediments are separated by interglacial deposits that formed during intervening milder spells. Typical rocks showing the features of glaciation—tillites and moraine deposits—of similar type and age are also found in northern Australia and in southeast Africa.

No further evidence for large-scale glaciation is then found until 940 million years ago; subsequent glacials occurred about 770 and 615 million years ago. After the Precambrian period, prominent glacial periods are known to have occurred during the late Ordovician and Permo-Carboniferous ages; then there was a long gap until the Pleistocene ice age.

Glacial rocks are preserved within rock sequences on continents such as Australia and in northern Africa—both currently enjoying dry, hot climates in low latitudes. Evidently the position of these continents has changed. For instance, the Permo-Carboniferous glaciation affected the whole of the huge "supercontinent" known as Pangea, which existed at that time. Subsequently Pangea split into Gondwanaland (the southern continents) and Laurasia (the northern), and was later further fragmented into the present-day continents. The record of past glaciations allows geologists to establish how the continents have moved around with respect to one another and to the poles.

Causes of glaciation

Exactly what causes a glaciation is not yet clear. Once it was thought that variations in the Sun's energy output were responsible; however, little is known about this. More likely are effects due to precession or changes in

Pangea

The vast supercontinent that came together on Earth during the latter part of Paleozoic time. Comprising all of the present-day continents, it finally fragmented in Mesozoic times.

Today glaciation is mainly focused at the poles, where huge icebergs originate, and in mountainous areas such as the Himalayas and Alps. During much of the Earth's history, even the polar regions were free from ice, being heated by warm sea currents.

the Earth's axis. Over long periods, changes occur in both the Earth's orbit and axial inclination. Precessional cycles occur every 26,000 years, 40,000 years, and 100,000 years. The English astronomer John Herschel first proposed precessional effects as an explanation in 1830. His ideas were refined in the 1930s by the Yugoslav Milutin Milankovitch.

Precession

Some support for such an idea comes from rock samples taken from deep ocean sediments and underlying crust, and also from the planet Mars. Precessional effects on Mars are much more significant than on Earth and might be expected to induce marked climatic variations. In the past, Mars enjoyed a milder climate during which there was running water and standing seas. Precession could explain the change. Other possible causes for global changes of temperature include natural phenomena such as large volcanoes. These have the capacity to lower global temperatures by several degrees, as the clouds of ash and gas they eject absorb the Sun's heat.

Global climate

There are a number of factors that can affect the global climate. Not all of these are cyclic or periodic and some have a greater effect than others, but all of them can lead to an ice age.

First, plate tectonics make the continents drift. The position of the continents affects the movement of warm water around the planet, regarded by most scientists to be Earth's equivalent of a home's central heating system. The system has been termed the global conveyor. When the movement of continents alters water patterns, the flow of heat around the planet is disrupted and, if less heat is channeled from the equator to the higher latitudes, there may be an onset of an ice age.

Precession

The slow movement of the celestial poles. It is largely due to the wobbling motion of the Earth's rotational axis induced by gravitational attraction of the Moon on Earth's equatorial bulge.

Second, the process of mountain building can disrupt the atmospheric circulation patterns. This can have a similar effect as the changing of the ocean circulation. For example, the recent uplift of the Himalayas and the Tibetan plateau, along with a global average rise of continental height by 1800 feet (600 meters) during the last 15 million years, have probably contributed to the current ice age.

Third, the proportion of carbon dioxide in the atmosphere can influence the global climate. Antarctic ice cores can be analyzed to show the carbon dioxide content of the atmosphere throughout geological time, and they indicate a close correlation between the lack of carbon dioxide in the atmosphere and ice ages. Periods of time when there have been large quantities of carbon dioxide have produced "greenhouse" warming of the Earth and kept the ice ages at bay. A growing number of scientists believe the increasing quantity of carbon dioxide, currently being placed into the atmosphere by human acitvity, is going to exceed natural levels so much that the polar caps will melt. The freshwater released could

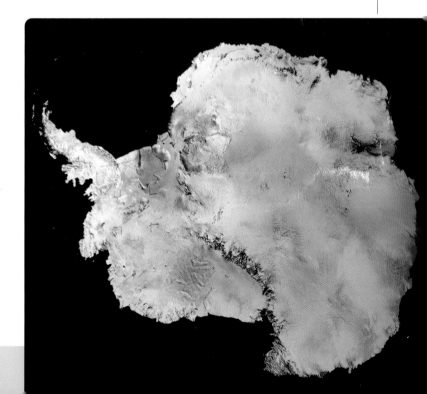

The continent of Antarctica is currently a very important factor in the global climate because it sits over the South Pole. It is 5 million square miles (12.5 million square kilometers) in area, and the central plateau rises to an altitude of over 9800 feet (3000 meters.)

shut off the global conveyor completely and that would plunge Earth into another glaciation.

Whereas these factors are not periodically repeating events, there is now a large amount of evidence to suggest that the ice ages of the last few million years have been triggered, and subsequently overcome, by the amount of solar radiation our planet receives as a result of cyclic variations in the Earth's orbit.

The Milankovitch cycle

During the 1930s, Milutin Milankovitch, a Serbian scientist, presented the theory that three distinct variations in Earth's orbit could contribute to the ice ages. First, the Earth's orbit gradually changes from a circle to an elliptical path and back again, over a time period of 100,000 years. Second and third, its rotational

The Milankovitch cycles are made up of three components. First, the Earth's rotation axis wobbles, causing it to point in different directions. Second, the axis changes angle between 24.5 to 21.5 degrees. Finally, the Earth's orbit varies between being a circle and an ellipse.

Precession today

Earth Sun

At aphelion,
(farthest from the Sun),
Northern Hemisphere
is tilted toward Sun

23,000 years ago

At aphelion,
Northern Hemisphere
is tilted away from Sun

Obliquity today

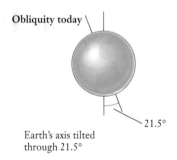

21.5°

Earth's axis tilted
through 21.5°

40,000 years a

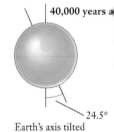

24.5°

Earth's axis tilted
through 24.5°

Orbital eccentricity today

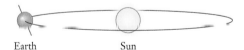

Earth Sun

100,000 years ago

axis changes from 24.5 to 21.5 degrees and wobbles (precesses) around in a circle. The change of the Earth's tilt (obliquity) takes about 40,000 years and the precession 23,000. Together they create a complex cycle of changes to both the amount of radiation the Earth receives and where it enters the planet. They have been linked strongly to the advance and retreat of the ice sheets during the most recent ice age.

In addition, global changes of temperature could be caused by the natural equivalent of nuclear winters. This term refers to the clouds of dust that a nuclear war would blow up into the atmosphere. The dust would block out the sunlight, causing global temperatures to plummet. A similar scenario could be imagined from extensive volcanic eruptions or from the impact of a comet or asteroid. Such events could also cause ice ages.

The gradual rise of the Himalayan mountain range has affected the global circulation of air currents and is probably partly responsible for the onset of the most recent ice age. Mount Everest on the left and its summit have been blown clear of snow by winds from the jetstream.

Obliquity

The angle that one plane makes with another. For instance, the ecliptic makes an angle of 23° 26′ with the celestial equator (because the Earth's equator is inclined at this angle to the orbital plane). This is termed the obliquity of the ecliptic.

Mobile and Stable Zones

The Earth has existed for about 4.6 billion years. During this time, the patterns of land and sea have changed across the entire planet. New crustal rocks have been continually created; some have been on the surface for a very long time, others less so; still others have been destroyed and recycled.

A quick glance at a modern map of the world shows that if the continents were cut out like the pieces in a huge jigsaw, many could be roughly fitted together. This was first remarked upon as long ago as 1620. In 1912 the Austrian meteorologist Alfred Wegener published a book in which he noted similarities in ancient fossil remains between the rocks of western Africa and eastern South America. This, he argued, could not be mere concidence; might it not mean that the two continents were once joined?

This idea was not taken seriously until the late 1950s and early 1960s, when new techniques in geochemistry and geophysics—as well as the traditional methods of paleontology and stratigraphy—produced a breakthrough. It became evident that Wegener had been right, and the continents had in fact drifted. A further new understanding was that Earth's lithosphere is segmented and that the individual pieces, or plates, are in constant motion.

Lithosphere

The rigid outermost layer of a planet. On Earth, it lies above the asthenosphere and includes the crust and upper part of the mantle, and is approximately 60 miles (100 km) in depth. The Earth's lithosphere is segmented into plates.

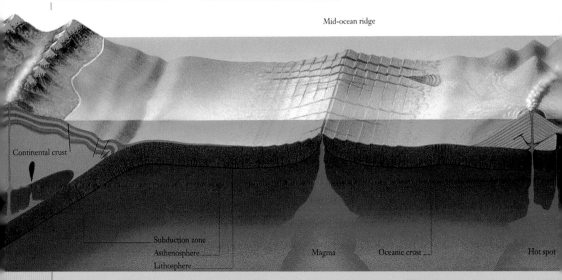

Mid-ocean ridge

Continental crust

Subduction zone
Asthenosphere
Lithosphere

Magma   Oceanic crust   Hot spot

Mobile zones

Most of the Earth's crust is geologically stable most of the time. Intense geological activity is confined to narrow linear zones, called mobile zones, that correspond to plate margins; volcanoes, earthquakes, and mountain-building occur here. Between them are extensive, relatively flat, stable zones.

Each of the stable continental regions is built from several components. Thus, extensive regions of interior Australia and North America are quite flat and have remained essentially undisturbed since Precambrian times—from the Earth's formation more than four billion years ago. The ancient cratonic core of Australia underlies the central and western part of the continent. Its components are separated by belts of past mountain-building activity. Sedimentary rocks covering

Curriculum Context

The student is expected to research and describe the historical development of the theories of plate tectonics, including continental drift and sea-floor spreading.

Underneath the Ocean

The crust beneath the oceans is punctured by long ridges, where new crust is being created. Magnetic alignments "frozen" in rock across mid-oceanic ridges and radiometric dating both reveal that the age of the sea-floor rocks increases away from ridge axes. As the oceanic crust moves over mantle hotspots, chains of volcanic islands may form, and where it encounters the continents it is driven downward (subducted), to be recycled through the mantle. The subduction zones may involve regions of complex mountain-building, which eventually cause the area of the continental crust to extend. These "crustal plate" movements form the theory of plate tectonics.

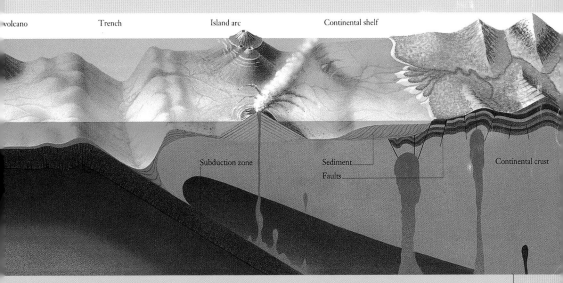

volcano   Trench   Island arc   Continental shelf

Subduction zone   Sediment   Continental crust
Faults

the craton provide evidence for almost continuous undisturbed sedimentation for more than 1.5 billion years in this region. This is the hallmark of a stable zone.

Orogenisis

Volcanoes and earthquakes disrupt the crust on a local scale but form a part of a much more widespread phenomenon—orogenesis (mountain building). Terrestrial fold mountains are formed by complex processes that occur at the margins of plates in collision (destructive plate margins). Oceanic crust and its veneer of sediments are subducted or driven down into the mantle and buried. They then heat up, melt, deform, and undergo metamorphism, leading to the eventual rise of new mountain chains from the sea.

Mobile zones

Mobile zones are separated from one another by stable ones. An overview of the Earth reveals that orogenic belts form the boundaries of the continents and have been periodically accreted to continental cores. The history of mobile belts is cyclic. Periods of relative calm are offset by periods of mountain-building that have changed the appearance of the face of the Earth.

Igneous activity

Mountain-building involves volcanism, magmatism, and seismic activity—collectively called igneous activity. Because it involves all these processes, the history of an individual orogenic belt may be very complex. There have been peaks in igneous activity at certain times—2.8 through 2.6 billion years ago, 1.9 through 1.6 billion years ago, 1.1 billion through 900 million years ago, and about 500 million years ago—suggesting that the Earth's heat engine needs to build up energy before another cycle can begin.

Divergent plate margins, where two plates move away from each other, also are active zones. Material from

Metamorphism
The process that changes existing rocks mineralogically, but without them entering the liquid phase—that is, without melting.

The Pacific Rim

The mobile regions of the Earth are delineated by zones of intense earthquake activity, particularly around the margins of the Pacific Ocean, where they are accompanied by deep subduction trenches. Seismicity is also concentrated along oceanic ridges but is not so intense. Active volcanism typifies both types of active region, which mark the contacts between adjacent lithospheric plates. Isolated oceanic islands are also active regions within otherwise stable zones. These are associated with "hot spots." The stable regions separate the mobile zones and comprise the continental interiors and the abyssal plains of the ocean basins.

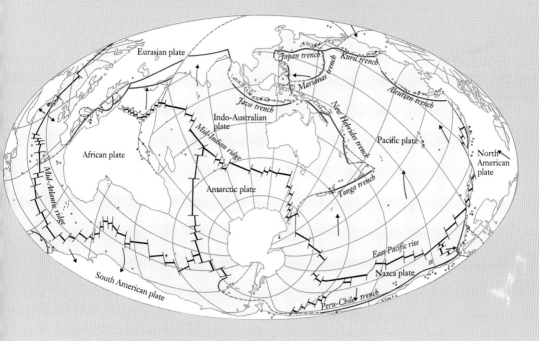

the mantle wells up to approach the surface beneath oceanic ridges; major rifting, hydration (swelling in minerals that have taken water into their structure), and eruption of lavas occurs. Magma is intruded into the subcrust as dikes and sheets.

Wandering Continents

There is good evidence for continental drift—the theory of the Earth's development that presents the modern continents as interlocking components of an ancient supercontinent that began to break up about 200 million years ago.

One such piece of evidence is the structure of the Saharan shield in Africa. This 2-billion-year-old craton has a strong north–south grain in its interior, but this swings toward an east–west trend along the Atlantic margin. There is a well-defined junction between the ancient rocks and younger ones; this strikes into the ocean off the coast of Ghana. The geological features along the eastern coast of South America reveal almost identical relationships in Brazil. From these, it is clear that the two continents were once joined and have drifted apart. Similar evidence occurs on other continents.

Paleontological evidence

Then there is paleontological evidence. Fossil remains collected from Africa and Greenland indicate that, during Silurian times (430 million years ago), Africa was in the grip of glaciation (cold temperatures and extended ice cover), whereas Greenland had a tropical climate. Each must have changed latitude—quite dramatically. Again, evidence of similar changes of climatic conditions is found on other continents.

Paleomagnetism

One of the most convincing arguments for continental drift is from paleomagnetism. It is known that the Earth's magnetic polarity varies and sometimes reverses. Magnetic minerals trapped inside rocks take on the magnetic polarity of their era. Geophysicists can use this phenomenon to determine their paleolatitude by using simple trigonometry. Once they have this information, they can establish the past magnetic orientation of any

Continental Drift

A theory, generally attributed to Alfred Wegener, postulating the early existence of a single ancient supercontinent that eventually broke up, beginning to drift apart about 200 million years ago.

continent. Plots of paleopole positions for older and older rocks from any one continent define a smooth curve (called a polar wandering curve), which leads away from the present pole. One possible interpretation is that the position of the magnetic pole has changed. However, wandering curves for different continents over similar periods of time do not coincide. This suggests that it is not the magnetic pole but the continents themselves that have moved.

Attempting to reconstruct the positions of continents at the start of the Paleozoic era is not easy. Nevertheless, most geologists agree that North America and Greenland should be put back together and placed alongside western Europe. This part of the jigsaw is called Laurasia. At the same time, Africa has to be placed alongside South America. Australasia,

Paleopole

The last position of the Earth's magnetic poles as determined in rocks from their remnant magnetization.

Moving Continents

At the start of Paleozoic times there was a single supercontinent called Pangea, which stretched from pole to pole. A single ocean, Panthalassa, encircled it. By the Carboniferous (350 million years ago), a southern supercontinent, Gondwanaland had moved over the South Pole, while ancestral China, Laurasia, and Siberia formed separate northern continents. Laurasia included pieces of what eventually formed North America. By the Permian (250 million years ago), the continents had come together again, reforming Pangea. The Tethys Sea separated the northern and southern parts, and this opened to the east. In the Cenozoic, drift of the continents occurred again. Gondwanaland separated from Laurasia, and both split up.

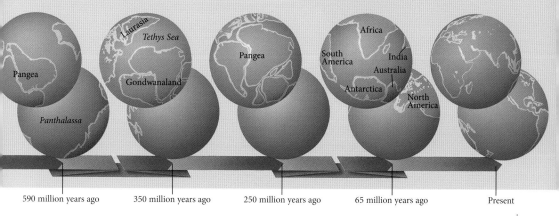

| Pangea | Laurasia | | | | |

Panthalassa

Tethys Sea

Gondwanaland

Pangea

Africa

South America

India

Australia

Antarctica

North America

| 590 million years ago | 350 million years ago | 250 million years ago | 65 million years ago | Present |

Curriculum Context

The student is expected to use current theories to design and construct a geological time scale.

India, and Antarctica can be convincingly pieced together on the basis of fossil, structural, and paleomagnetic data during the Early Paleozoic—somewhat sooner than the pieces of Laurasia. By the late Paleozoic (around 200 million years ago), however, Laurasia and the southern supercontinent, Gondwanaland, were united and formed a single vast continent, known as Pangea. At this time the eastern parts of Pangea were separated by a great ocean, known as Tethys, which was to remain a feature of the Earth for many millions of years.

During Triassic times (about 220 million years ago), the north magnetic pole lay in Alaska, while the southern pole was situated just off the coast of Antarctica. Then, between 160 and 120 million years ago, the supercontinent gradually split apart as new oceans began to form between the Americas, Africa, and India, and Africa and South America. By about 80 million years ago, Australia and New Zealand—previously joined—became separated. It was not until 40 million years ago, however, that Australia finally split itself from Antarctica and drifted away from the pole.

Continental shields have been stable for hundreds of millions of years. But they have moved large distances due to continental drift. Ayres Rock (Uluru), in the center of Australia, is a remnant of Precambrian glacial deposits formed when Australia was close to the South Pole.

Plates and Plumes

New crust is continually generated at mid-ocean ridges and this causes the Earth's continents to move around. However, the Earth is neither expanding nor contracting; therefore, if a balance is to be kept, somewhere crust must be being destroyed. The theory of plate tectonics was developed to explain how this might come about and how the continents drift around the globe.

In the early 1900s, the idea of continental drift was viewed with skepticism, because no one could imagine how the mantle (which was proved by seismic waves to be solid) might carry slabs of lithosphere from place to place. Then the German-American geophysicist Beno Gutenberg (1889–1960) demonstrated that the mantle, although of extreme viscosity, could still have convective currents within it. This was a key step forward.

Scientists began to probe the ocean floors in the mid-20th century, using geophysical techniques and deep-sea coring and sampling. As a result, vital pieces of geological evidence came to light to show that the ocean floors, like the continents, were in motion. It could then be shown that the lithosphere of the Earth is composed of seven very large and a number of smaller plates which behave as if they were rigid and which are pushed around by movements within the mantle that are transmitted along the asthenosphere.

The mantle was considered to be in convective motion, with upwelling mantle found along the lines in mid-ocean, known as spreading axes. The hot mantle generates magma which is lighter than its surroundings and so rises toward the surface. As it does so it cools, crystallizes, and moves sideways away from spreading axes. The cooling induces contraction, with the result that the spreading axes form ridges

Convection

The mechanism of heat transfer within a flowing material, in which hot material from lower levels rises because it is less dense. The movement is complemented by the sinking of cooler material from near the surface.

Curriculum Context

Students should know the principal structures that form at the three different kinds of plate boundaries.

The formation of a chain of islands begins with a single shield volcano above a mantle hot spot (1). Volcanic activity may continue at this site for several million years, and the volcano will eventually emerge at sea level, creating a new island.

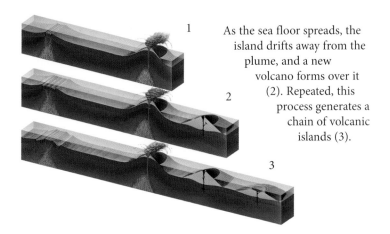

As the sea floor spreads, the island drifts away from the plume, and a new volcano forms over it (2). Repeated, this process generates a chain of volcanic islands (3).

above the rest of the ocean floor, which subsides. Destruction of the lithosphere takes place along long, narrow zones called subduction zones. Here, spreading lithosphere plunges down, at angles of about 45°, beneath an opposing plate, to be heated, melted and recycled in the Earth's interior. Sometimes, however, two continental plates converge. In this case the two may be thrust together to buckle and form mountain ranges, rather than subducted. India and Asia have done this along the line of the Himalayas, thrusting together slices of brittle crust.

As the Indian plate approached the Eurasian plate, the sedimentary rocks of the ocean crust were compressed and thrust up to form the rugged Himalaya mountain range.

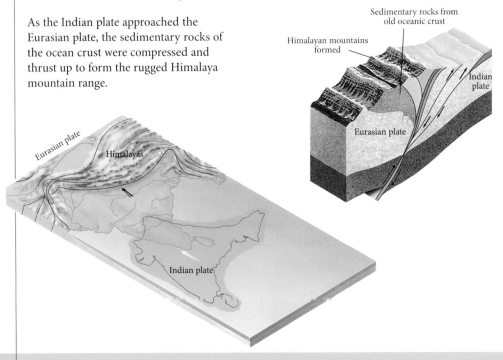

Sedimentary rocks from old oceanic crust

Himalayan mountains formed

Indian plate

Eurasian plate

Eurasian plate

Himalayas

Indian plate

Beneath the Ocean Floor

Since the late 1930s, new techniques have opened up the field of submarine geology. Gravity measurements and geotectonic imagery—in which very accurate measurements of the height of the sea surface allow the bottom structure of the oceans to be mapped—have greatly increased our understanding.

Mid-ocean ridges

The ocean floor, far from being smooth and flat, is crossed by enormous mountain ranges which rise 1–2 miles (2–3 kilometers) above the general level of the sea floor and form part of a global network which extends for more than 49,500 miles (80,000 kilometers). These are the mid-oceanic ridges. In places such as Iceland, Ascension, and the Galápagos Islands, ridges rise above sea level. The ocean floor is also cut by deep trenches which mark subduction zones and it is punctuated by isolated seamounts.

Constructive plate margins

The discovery of what mid-oceanic ridge systems represented—the sites of crust formation, or constructive plate margins—was a major breakthrough in earth science. Basaltic volcanism—the upwelling of magma consisting mainly of basalt—characterizes oceanic ridges. Convective movements within the mantle force the overlying lithosphere to move apart, allowing hot magma to reach the sea floor. At ridge crests, a zone of rifting separates regions of sea floor, which are moving apart at 1–6 inches (2–15 centimeters) per year. Because the oceanic crust cannot withstand sufficient stress to allow for variations in spreading rate and changes in convection pattern, oceanic ridges consist of straight sections offset by transform faults, along which different sections of a plate slide past each other.

Polarity reversal

The Earth's magnetic field episodically shows reversals in its polarity, giving rise to magnetic epochs of normal and reversed polarity. Reversals occur at intervals of between 10,000 and 25 million years and give rise to magnetic striping in rocks.

The Mid-Atlantic Ridge

One of the key pieces of information came from paleomagnetic studies along the Mid-Atlantic Ridge. It was found that only half the rocks on each side of the ridge axis near Iceland showed normal magnetic polarity; the remainder had a reversed polarity (a magnetic needle would point south). The pattern of normal and reversed polarity was manifested in a magnetic striping of the oceanic crust, mirrored on each side of the ridge crest. When individual stripes were dated, it was found that the rocks became older with increasing distance from the crest. In other words, the sea floor was spreading apart. Such spreading characterizes all oceanic ridges where lithospheric plate divergence occurs. During the past 80 million years, the Atlantic has spread at a rate of 1 inch (2.5 centimeters) per year.

Even more exciting discoveries have come from an international drilling project, the Deep Sea Drilling Project. Since 1968, a drill ship, the *Glomar Challenger*, has drilled nearly a thousand holes into the deep ocean basins, taking samples of deep-sea sediment and crust. One early discovery suggests that the Mediterranean dried up completely between 5 and 12 million years ago, leaving thick beds of sun-baked salts as evidence buried in today's ocean floor.

Iceland lies on the northern edge of the Mid-Atlantic Ridge, called the Reykjanes Ridge. This is one of the few locations on Earth where a ridge rises to the surface, so that volcanic activity along the ridge results in eruptions visible above the ocean surface, rather than thousands of feet below.

Island Arcs

Chains of islands cover the Pacific Ocean, the largest on Earth. They stretch from New Zealand in the southeast, through Tonga, Indonesia, the Philippines, and Japan, to the Aleutian islands off the coast of Alaska. This region is known as the "Ring of Fire" because of the intense seismic and volcanic activities that take place there; Indonesia alone has 150 active volcanoes.

The arcs are formed by volcanic activity where two sections of crust collide. Most island arcs occur at the margins of the Pacific, though small ones exist in the Atlantic and in the Mediterranean Sea. On the sides of the islands that face the interior of the ocean are found deep trenches up to 620 miles (1000 kilometers) long. One Pacific trench, the Mariana trench, is more than 36,000 feet (11,000 meters) deep—the deepest point anywhere on Earth, and twice the depth of the average ocean basin. The trenches are usually steeper on the side that faces a continent, and those in the Pacific are usually deeper than those in the Atlantic. Trenches are formed when colliding plates bring oceanic crust into contact with less dense continental crust; the oceanic crust is pushed down toward the mantle.

Discoveries about the processes that formed modern arcs have made it possible to recognize the rocks of island arcs that were active tens or hundreds of millions of years ago. This enables geologists to trace the pattern of plate movements and gain a clearer perception of how continents grow. They have shown that island arcs develop through volcanic activity, and tend to be composed of granodiorite (coarse igneous rock similar to granite), which resembles continental rock and is very different from the oceanic crust. This is true even in the Aleutian islands, off the coast of Alaska, where an island arc has been formed by the collision of two plates of oceanic crust. This implies that

Island Arc Formation

Island arcs form when moving plates of the lithosphere collide. As one plate is pushed beneath the other (subducted) (1), some of the crust melts, forming magma. This pushes up to the surface as a volcano, which eventually forms an island. Sediments collect, and as plate movements continue, the ocean basin diminishes as the continents on either side come closer together (2), with the island arc accreting to one side as more sediment builds up. Eventually the ocean basin may close (3) and a mountain range comprising deformed sedimentary and metamorphic rock is formed.

Subduction
Trench

Sediments

Ocean basin

Volcanic
island

Mountain
range

Magma

1

2

3

the processes that create island arcs are very different from other geological activity that occurs in mid-ocean, such as the volcanic islands that form over "hot spots" in the Earth's mantle.

Accretion

The enlargement of a continent by the tectonic addition of other crustal fragments.

An island arc can eventually accrete onto the nearby continent. The Indonesian arc has grown where the plate carrying Australia northward is being subducted beneath the plate that is bringing Southeast Asia southeastward. Eventually, when the two plates meet, all of the intervening oceanic crust will have been consumed between them, forming a continental rather than an island arc. The rocks of the new arc will then collide with mainland Asia, leading to a complex sequence of events, involving deformation, magmatism, and metamorphism, by which they will be accreted on to the edge of the continent of Asia.

Earthquake zones

The study of island arcs allows geologists to predict the inevitable eruptions and earthquakes in these regions. Earthquakes near a trench tend to be shallow, and the seismic foci become progressively deeper on the continental side of it. This observation has allowed Benioff zones—seismically active planes inclined at about 45°—to be defined. These planes represent the area in which oceanic crust is actively being subducted. The discovery of Benioff zones provided important evidence for subduction caused by plate collision.

Benioff zone

The steeply inclined zone of seismic activity that extends downward from an oceanic trench toward the asthenosphere. Named for H. Benioff, a designer of musical instruments and seismographs. Such zones mark the path of a tectonic plate being subducted at a destructive plate margin.

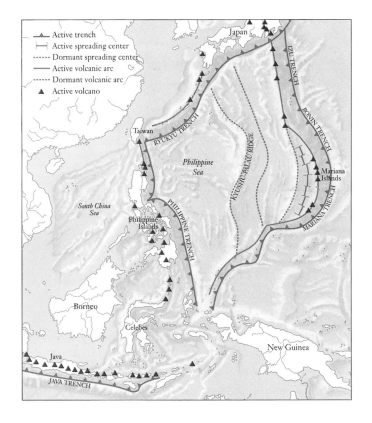

The Mariana, Philippine, and Ryukyu trenches are moving west as the Pacific Ocean crust is pushed under Asia. Between the Philippine and the Mariana trenches lies an inactive region where, about 25 million years ago, a new mountain ridge and ocean basin appeared and then became extinct.

Mountains from the Sea

Where lithospheric plates converge, compressional stresses result. Sedimentary rocks that have accumulated near continental margins or alongside island arcs may be dismembered by massive submarine landslides triggered during subduction and collision. As they are carried deeper into the Earth, they become crumpled as if held in a huge vise. In this way, a complex sequence of events begins, culminating in the formation of fold mountain chains: the process of orogenesis.

Orogenesis

The tectonic process that produces fold belts, metamorphism, and magmatism, typically from a sequence of sedimentary rocks that have been involved in plate convergence. The culmination of an orogeny is the uprise of new belts of fold mountains.

The Andes mountain chain runs along the length of the western seaboard of South America. These comparatively young mountains have resulted from the Nazca plate—which carries a part of the Pacific ocean floor—being overridden by and subducted beneath the westward-moving South American plate, which has continental South America on its leading edge. Deep trenches have formed offshore and the oceanic plate dips down at 25° beneath the continent. Some 186 miles (300 kilometers) east of the trench line, the foothills of the Andes rise to their summits, the sites of numerous active volcanoes.

The Andean ranges are characterized by linear chains of intensely deformed rocks that were laid down before Mesozoic times and folded in the Late Mesozoic. Deeply buried sedimentary rocks becme deformed and recrystallized to form metamorphic rocks, while large volumes of magma pushed upward to create batholiths made of granite. These were less dense than their surroundings, and so added buoyancy to the continental margin. The latest phase of mountain-building took place during Late Neogene times (10 million years ago). Earthquakes and volcanic activity have continued until today.

Inland from the north Pacific coast, similar movements formed the Cascades and other northern cordilleras. Today, however, the northwest-moving Pacific plate has lost ground to the westward-moving North American plate. North of the Gulf of California, the boundary is offset by transform faults, such as the San Andreas Fault. There is no deep trench here, and earthquake foci are near the surface. These characteristics have arisen since North America overrode the eastern Pacific floor, so that the "mid-oceanic" ridge now lies beneath continental America. A triple junction formed where the East Pacific plate, the current Pacific plate, and the

Creating the Cordilleras

Adjacent to the Andean coast of western South America, the South American plate is advancing westward and overriding the Nazca plate, located to its west. The latter is virtually stationary and carries part of the Pacific ocean floor. Deep trenches run parallel to the plate boundary and are located almost immediately above the contact. A Benioff zone slopes at around 25 percent eastward under the continent. Frequent earthquakes characterize this zone. Approximately 185 miles (300 kilometers) east of this line, the foothills of the Andean cordilleras rise from

the coastal plain. Active volcanism is a feature of this impressive chain, magmas being generated where the subducted oceanic plate has reached sufficient depths for melting to take place. The Nazca plate is being subducted at a rate of 4 inches (10 cm) per year.

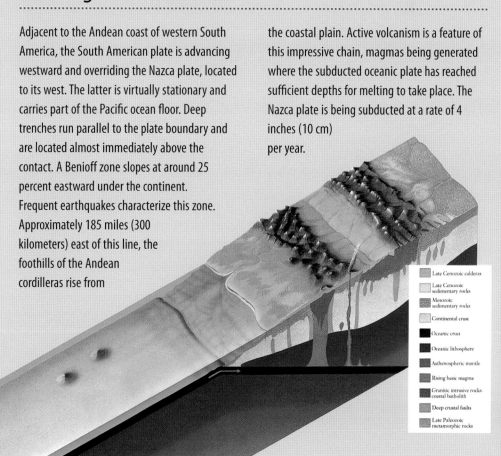

Late Cenozoic calderas

Late Cenozoic sedimentary rocks

Mesozoic sedimentary rocks

Continental crust

Oceanic crust

Oceanic lithosphere

Asthenospheric mantle

Rising basic magma

Granitic intrusive rocks: coastal batholith

Deep crustal faults

Late Paleozoic metamorphic rocks

An aerial view of the Himalaya mountain chain, formed when the Indian plate collided with the Eurasian plate. This range of mountains contains the highest peak on Earth.

North American plate meet. This unstable plate contact is slowly migrating up the continental margin.

The highest range of mountains on Earth, the Himalayas, was formed where the continents of India and Asia collided about 40 million years ago. Before this, fold mountains of similar age to the Alps (formed during Tertiary times) existed at the same site. The continental crust beneath the Himalayas is about 43 miles (70 kilometers thick), about twice the average thickness. This is because continental crust does not subduct easily, and collision pressures were absorbed not by folding, but by the stacking up of huge rock slices along low-angled faults, which are called thrusts.

Rift Valleys

Fifty million years ago, the island of Madagascar began to split off from the African continent. Today Africa is still being torn apart from the Red Sea and Jordan valley, through Ethiopia, and across Kenya as far south as the borders of South Africa.

This area, known as the mighty East African Rift Valley, is a 3000-mile- (5000-kilometer-) long zone of fracturing that began to form during the mid-Tertiary (about 30 million years ago) by stretching associated with continental drift. The same process caused the supercontinent Gondwanaland to break up 100 million years earlier.

Continents break up along the lines of faults—weak points in their structure caused by geological movement that fractures rocks. The subsiding of the land along the faults eventually forms a rift valley. A block of planetary crust drops down between the faults. This is called graben. It is often accompanied by a block of upfaulted crust, called horst. These contrasting blocks produce the characteristic valleys and peaks of rift valleys.

The East African Rift Valley

A major feature of the eastern side of the African continent was a broad dome of planetary crust (which still occupies most of Kenya). This rose in response to hot mantle material rising up beneath the continental crust, which began to stretch during Tertiary times. The rift faulting peaked during Miocene times, 25 through 5 million years ago. It was accompanied by volcanic activity, which has continued to the present. Not surprisingly, the rift is an area of above-average heat flow from the Earth's interior, and volcanic activity and faulting continue to tear apart this side of Africa at a rate of 1 inch (2.5cm) per year.

Graben

A downfaulted block of crust bordered by a pair of normal faults, caused by extensional deformation. Graben formation is common on the crest and flanks of rising crustal domes, such as the Kenya Dome in East Africa.

The main rift faults are as much as 10,000 feet (3000 meters) deep in Tanzania, and the rift itself—which splits in two around Lake Victoria—is up to 125 miles (200 kilometers wide). The movement of the crust has resulted in volcanic activity, giving rise to large volumes of flat-lying basalt and phonolite flows and a number of large stratovolcanoes (volcanoes with a distinctive conical shape), including Africa's highest mountain, Kilimanjaro.

Rift Valley Development

The initial stage in rift valley development (1) is the upward arching of the crust caused by rising plumes of mantle material. The zone of potential splitting is one of high heat flow and seismic activity (2). Melting of rocks below the crust generates magmas. Because the overlying lithosphere has been stretched and thinned, these gain easy access to the surface. Sheets of lava are extruded on the rift floor and flanks. Vertical faulting takes place (3). As extension continues, the rift widens, and a series of normal faults develop. The throw on these may be a mile (1.6 km) or more. Volcanic activity becomes more centralized and, because magmas have to penetrate continental-type crust, any volcanoes tend to be highly explosive.

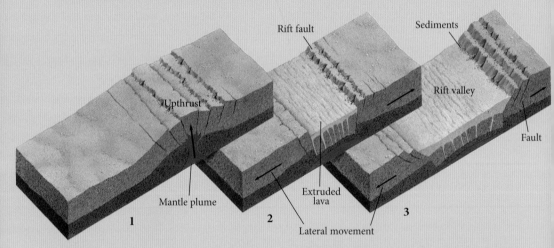

Rifts and volcanic activity are typical of regions where mantle material is rising under the lithosphere. The most extensive of all terrestrial rift faults are found along oceanic ridge systems.

If Africa continues to split apart at its present rate (about 1 inch, or 2.5 cm, per year) eventually a new ocean will flow into the rifted region and a new continent will form.

Geological Stories

Geological time has been split into a number of major divisions: eons, eras, epochs, and periods. The earliest eon is the Archean, which spans the period between the birth of the Solar System, about 4.6 billion years ago, through 2.5 billion years ago. Evidence for mountain-building in this period is to be found within Earth's rocks, as well as volcanism and deposition of marine sediments. Although the Archean was once defined as the period before life existed, simple life forms are now known to have existed toward the end of this period.

The Archean was followed by the Proterozoic (which means period of first life), which extended until about 590 million years ago. Again, periods of mountain-building punctuated periods of lesser activity and, during the latter part of the Proterozoic, more complex life forms developed in the primeval oceans. Together these two eons comprise the period of time known as the Precambrian. Throughout this time the Earth's continental crust was never more than 25 miles (40 kilometers) thick—considerably less than the modern crust, which can be up to 43 miles (70 kilometers) thick.

During the Archean eon the Earth's crust was repeatedly bombarded by meteoroids and asteroids. This also happened on Mercury, the Moon, and Mars, and, indeed, on the moons of the outer planets, which are intensely cratered. Samples of Moon rock brought back by the Apollo astronauts show that lunar activity, including volcanic filling of the Moon's maria, had virtually finished by the end of Archean times; this is probably true of Mercury too. Mars and Venus, in contrast, have remained geologically active well into more recent times.

Life on Earth began to multiply and diversify at the beginning of the Cambrian period (590–505 million

Curriculum Context

Students should know that the evidence from geological studies of Earth and other planets suggests that the early Earth was very different from Earth today.

Archean

The earliest part of Precambrian time, extending from the birth of the Earth as a planet through 2500 million years ago. Rocks of this age do not generally contain fossil remains.

years ago), the first of a series of geological periods which comprise the Phanerozoic (eon of life). By Cambrian times it appears that volcanism on Mars was well past its peak; however, resurfacing of Venus by volcanic activity seems to have continued beyond that point, and possibly continued until the present time.

Curriculum Context

Students should know the evidence for the existence of planets orbiting other stars and the likelihood of other life forms being found there.

Because the Universe is so large, the number of stars resembling our Sun is very high, and many scientists consider the likelihood that the conditions for life to emerge on other planets in other parts of the Universe is likely. However, no such planets have yet been found, and no signs of life have been found on the other planets in our own Solar System.

Mammals evolve

The first mammals evolved over 200 million years ago, but their domination of the Earth may have been assisted by a collision between an asteroid and the Earth about 65 million years ago, causing the extinction of the hugely successful dinosaurs. Had this not taken place, humans might not now be in their privileged position: the earliest ancestors of the human race did not emerge, until the Pliocene epoch, no more than four or five million years ago, probably in East Africa.

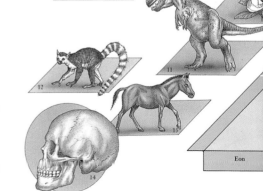

1	Shelled organisms	8	Early mammals
2	Early jawless fish	9	First birds
3	Tree ferns, horsetails	10	Flowering plants
4	Air-breathing fish	11	Last dinosaurs
5	Large amphibians	12	First primates
6	Early reptiles	13	Early horses
7	Ginkgos, conifers	14	Modern humans

Evolution on Earth

The geological timescale is based on obvious changes in rock type of fossil groups from one period to the next. The major divisions are the eons, which are divided into eras and further broken down into periods and, for the most recent era, covering the last 65 million years, epochs. The Precambrian era encompasses about four-fifths of the Earth's entire history. The end of the Precambrian era was marked by the appearance of the first fossils. Major life forms developed through the major periods, starting with the Cambrian; jawless fish emerged in the Ordovician period (505–438 million years ago); the first land plants were found in the Silurian (438–408 million years ago); and the first amphibians during the Devonian (408–360 million years ago). The most recent Ice Age was in the Pleistocene and Holocene.

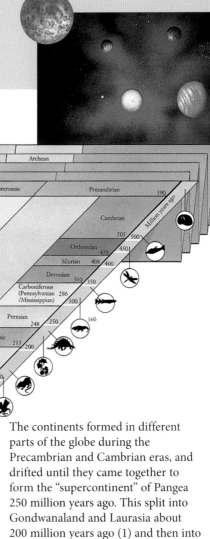

The continents formed in different parts of the globe during the Precambrian and Cambrian eras, and drifted until they came together to form the "supercontinent" of Pangea 250 million years ago. This split into Gondwanaland and Laurasia about 200 million years ago (1) and then into their present form (2).

Nothing Is Forever

Modern understanding of the history of the Earth has come largely from stratigraphy—the study of layers of rock. By studying the rocks being formed today, in known environments, geologists are able to infer what was happening in the distant past, interpreting each rock layer in the light of this knowledge.

Because life began in the sea and has continued to flourish there, the record of fossil remains within sedimentary strata also represents an evolutionary series. Thus stratigraphy is aided by paleontology, the study of fossils. Stratigraphic and paleontological studies of the rock record indicate that Earth's history moves in cycles, with periods of relative stability punctuated by upheaval. During the process of orogenesis, once-horizontal strata may be rucked up into fold mountains, while others may be completely destroyed by erosion, giving rise to gaps in the rock record. These gaps are called unconformities. These features can be seen in the Grand Canyon of Arizona.

The geological processes of today are similar to those of the past. However, the rate at which the processes take place may have changed. Time is very important in geology. Most changes occur very slowly, but sudden storms or volcanic eruptions may change the face of a region very quickly. These events are recorded by rocks.

Mineral content

A rock is a collection of minerals—solid materials with ordered atomic structures. Most rocks are silicates, consisting of various metallic cations (positive ions) in combination with silicon and oxygen, the latter usually in the form of the negative SiO_4^{4-} anion. Because of the different cations they contain, the various silicate minerals have diverse internal structures. Some are strongly bonded and therefore very hard; others have looser bonds and may be more susceptible to mechanical or chemical attack.

All minerals ultimately come from inside the planets, having crystallized during the cooling of molten magma. The crystals that form do so under considerable pressure and at temperatures ranging between 930°F or 500°C (in the case of granite) and 2000°F or 1100°C (in the case of basalt). As a result, if they reach the surface, they are not necessarily stable at the low temperatures and pressures found there. Furthermore, most have weaknesses in their structures, inherited from the way their atoms are bonded.

Rock weathering

At the Earth's surface, outcrops of rock are attacked by water, wind, and ice. Rocks are vulnerable to attack along inherent weaknesses such as bedding planes, joints, and fractures, and eventually pieces are broken off. In time they are transported elsewhere by a combination of gravity, running water, ice, and wind. As they do so, the fragments collide with each other and against other outcrops and are eventually broken into individual mineral grains. These destructive

Sandstone monoliths are found in the state of Utah, a region of North America that has been a stable zone in recent times. Recent stripping of the plateaulike landscape of Mesozoic sandy rocks has left residual mesas, buttes, and pinnacles, such as those of Arches National Park.

processes of weathering and erosion are followed by the deposition of the rock fragments as sedimentary layers, or strata.

Granite

The mineral quartz (SiO_2) is a major constituent of the granitic rocks which are typical of many continental interiors. Quartz is also extremely abundant in many of the sedimentary rocks derived from these and later deposited as sediments. It has a strong atomic structure, making it resistant to chemical attack. In this respect, quartz contrasts sharply with feldspar, another component of granite, whose crystals are weakened by the presence of cleavage planes (planes of weak bonding in the mineral's atomic lattice) and of molecules that are readily broken down by the weakly acidic rainwater. Feldspar grains, therefore, are steadily broken down and form clays, while some of their constituents dissolve and are carried away by streams and rivers, eventually to be recrystallized elsewhere. All other rock-forming silicates except quartz undergo similar degradation.

Quartz

One of the most widespread silicate minerals of the Earth's continental regions and the chief component in clastic sedimentary rocks. It is mostly silicon dioxide (SiO_2).

Components of Granite

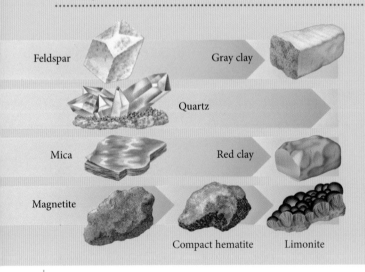

Feldspar

Gray clay

Quartz

Mica

Red clay

Magnetite

Compact hematite   Limonite

Weathering of granite produces feldspar, which converts to clays; quartz, which is is highly resistant; mica, which also breaks down to clays; and magnetite, the most common iron oxide, which is relatively insoluble and remains partly as opaque grains.

Sedimentation

The process of sedimentation, which occurs when the load of sediment carried by rivers (or glaciers) enters the sea or a lake, involves not only the deposition of layers of grains but also the eventual precipitation of mineral matter in solution. Sometimes this takes the form of a cement that crystallizes, after the sediment has been buried, from the water trapped between sediment grains. Processes occuring after deposition are important in converting separate grains into solid rocks, for instance, by the immense burial pressures that squeeze out pore water trapped between grains and push them closer together.

Many limestones are directly precipitated from seawater. They are made of calcium carbonate, which originated in reactions between atmospheric constituents such as carbon dioxide and carbonic acid in seawater. Carbonate is also fixed by marine organisms, which build their shells from it. The fixing of carbon dioxide into solid carbonate form has had the advantage of preventing buildup of the gas in the Earth's atmosphere; without it, a greenhouse effect like that found on Venus could have occurred on Earth and prevented the development of life.

Curriculum Context

The student is expected to demonstrate the density, hardness, streak, and cleavage of particular minerals.

The Work of Rivers

Rain may simply run off the Earth's surface or seep down into porous rocks to emerge at a lower level at a spring line; but eventually it feeds the tributary networks of rivers. These carry sediment and also deposit it along their courses, either as point bars within their channels or as debris spread out over the surrounding countryside in the form of flood deposits.

Water is collected into a river system by tributaries—a veinlike network of streams. In its upper reaches, slopes tend to be steep and the stream flows quickly; the river carries its load in suspension or by dragging larger debris along its bed. As it descends, it may pick up more load, but gradients lessen and the rate of flow diminishes; the rate of deposition increases. Where it finally disgorges into the sea or a lake, the river loses energy rapidly and deposits its load, resulting in a delta of sedimentary material through which the river must thread a new path.

The world's largest rivers, such as the Mississippi and Amazon, deliver huge quantities of water to the oceans: the Mississippi discharges 23,200 cubic yards (17,715 cubic meters) per second, but the Amazon disgorges ten times this volume. Each carries around a billion tons of sediments per year to the oceans. Beneath the modern delta of the Mississippi is a 3.7 mile- (6 km-) thick layer of sediments accumulated during the past 40 million years. At present, the river adds a further $\frac{1}{8}$ inch (1.5 millimeters) of new sediment to its delta each year.

Delta
The wedge-shaped body of sediment deposited by a river at its point of entry into an ocean or lake.

Moving Mississippi
The course of a major river system does not always remain the same. The Mississippi, for instance, during the Pleistocene Ice Age (up to 2 million years ago) when the sea levels were lower than today, cut itself a deep bed to compensate for the lowering in level.

When the ice melted and sea level rose again, the river dumped a broad sheet of coarse debris, then built up its banks and developed a more sinuous course. As each stage passed, it entered the sea at different points through channels of varying profile; the position and form of its deltas changed with time, producing a complex interleaving pattern of sedimentation.

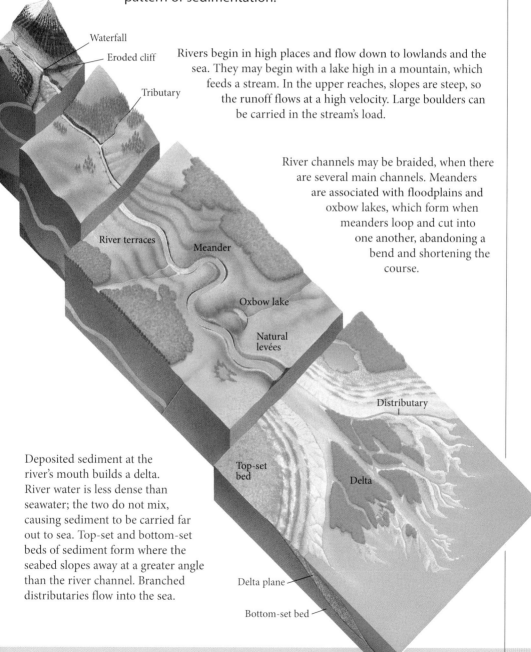

Waterfall

Eroded cliff

Tributary

Rivers begin in high places and flow down to lowlands and the sea. They may begin with a lake high in a mountain, which feeds a stream. In the upper reaches, slopes are steep, so the runoff flows at a high velocity. Large boulders can be carried in the stream's load.

River channels may be braided, when there are several main channels. Meanders are associated with floodplains and oxbow lakes, which form when meanders loop and cut into one another, abandoning a bend and shortening the course.

River terraces

Meander

Oxbow lake

Natural levées

Distributary

Deposited sediment at the river's mouth builds a delta. River water is less dense than seawater; the two do not mix, causing sediment to be carried far out to sea. Top-set and bottom-set beds of sediment form where the seabed slopes away at a greater angle than the river channel. Branched distributaries flow into the sea.

Top-set bed

Delta

Delta plane

Bottom-set bed

Seasonal rivers

In arid regions, rivers tend to flow only at certain seasons and may never reach the sea from interior deserts, instead depositing their sediment load in temporary lakes. Relatively small volumes of material are transported, but during violent storms substantial amounts of erosion and rapid movement of sediment may occur. Seasonal river flow is also typical of areas next to the polar ice caps. The main season of sediment transportation and deposition is the summer, when debris is freed from the ice.

The Zambezi River, the longest river in southern Africa at 1643 miles (2650 km), has an average flow as high as 21,000 cubic yards (16,000 cubic meters) per second. In Zimbabwe it spills over the magnificent Victoria Falls, shown here.

Coasts and Oceans

Surrounding the world's oceans are coastlines that stretch for hundreds of thousands of miles. They have been molded by the forces associated with the sea and hewn out of rocks of varying age and resilience. The sweep of shorelines is broken by the mouths of rivers, which bring sediment from the continental interiors to the oceans, often building extensive deltas at their mouths. The action of waves and currents may redistribute a proportion of this sediment along the neighboring coasts by a process called longshore drift.

Some shorelines are developing along rising continental margins. Isostatic adjustment or rebalancing that occurred after the retreat of Ice Age glaciers may have caused one part of the continent to rise; alternatively the margins themselves may be emerging from the oceans as a result of plate movements. Coastlines of emergence display active erosion as waves attack cliffs and raised beaches—the remains of old shorelines now lifted above sea level and backed by fossil cliffs. Conversely, coastlines of submergence occur where the land is sinking relative to sea level. They are found, for instance, along the southeast coast of Britain. Coastal plains may flood, leaving ridges and hills as islands near the shoreline.

Wave action

The power of sea waves is immense. The hydraulic action of waves pounding into joints and weaknesses within cliffs has the capacity literally to blow them apart; waves have been known to blast the roof out from a cave. This pounding action is rendered even more powerful by the debris that accumulates at the junction between land and sea. During storms and exceptionally high tides, sand and gravel enhance the scouring effect of waves and increase coastal erosion.

Isostacy
The principle that the rocks of the Earth's crust "float" on those of the underlying mantle.

Cliff erosion

Beach sediment is derived in part from rivers and their deltas, but also comes from cliff erosion. Where cliffs are built from soft rocks such as clays, slumping is common, erosion rapid, and material is removed relatively quickly. Tides tend to carry small mud-sized grains offshore before depositing them. Harder rocks are more resistant to attack and tend to form headlands. The pebbles and sand produced from such rocks stay close to the cliff base, forming beaches. Shelving beaches protect cliffs from erosion, because they absorb much of the power of breaking waves.

The margins of the continents slope gently under the waters of the ocean, forming continental shelves. In tropical latitudes, if sheltered conditions prevail, this shelf provides the ideal environment for the growth of coral which may build fringing reefs. Sometimes the coral growth on a sunken island produces an atoll or circular coral reef.

Seismic activity

In unstable regions, land-derived sediments which have built up at the edge of the continental shelf may be set in motion by seismic disturbances, which generate flows of sand, mud, and water called turbidity currents. These sweep down the continental slope onto the abyssal plains that extend oceanward, laying down sedimentary rocks known as turbidites. Turbidity currents off the coast of Newfoundland in the North

Margin

The edge of a tectonic plate, one of the huge slabs of the Earth's lithosphere that support the continents as they slowly drift around.

Turbidite

A sedimentary rock laid down by a turbidity current. A typical turbidite layer shows graded bedding and sedimentary "bottom structures," which are infills of grooves and hollows eroded into the sea bed by swiftly moving sediment-laden slurries.

Atlantic are particularly strong; they have broken trans-Atlantic telephone cables several times. Their activity may also help to cut deep canyons in the ocean floor along the continental margin.

On the deep sea floor, far from land, the only sediments that accumulate are organic oozes produced by marine algae and diatoms. This sediment is supplemented by volcanic dust which falls out of the atmosphere and slowly settles onto the abyssal plains.

Undersea earthquake

In 1929 an undersea earthquake off the Grand Bank of Newfoundland caused offshore sediment to slump, forming strong turbidity currents. The relatively dense suspensions prevented mixing with the water surrounding them, and the sediment spread across the sea floor at

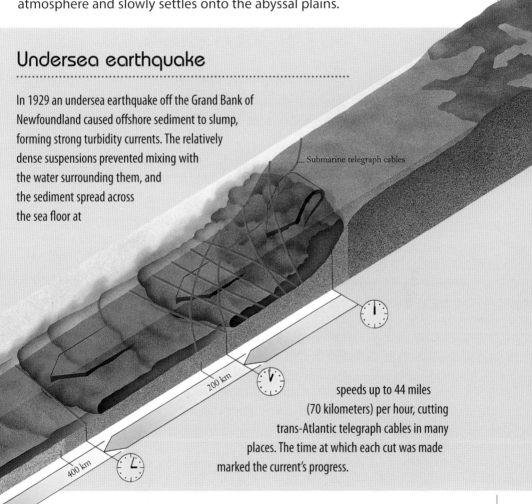

Submarine telegraph cables

200 km

400 km

speeds up to 44 miles (70 kilometers) per hour, cutting trans-Atlantic telegraph cables in many places. The time at which each cut was made marked the current's progress.

Deserts and Winds

Where global atmospheric circulation brings dry air down from the upper atmosphere (troposphere), deserts may develop. These are found both in hot regions at low altitudes (20–30° north or south of the Equator) and in cold ones next to polar ice caps.

Near the ice, the sediments are derived from shrinking glaciers, and surface features such as stone polygons may develop in response to freeze-thaw activity. In hot deserts such as the Sahara, extensive "sand seas" or ergs grow in response to accumulations of wind-blown sand, forming dune fields. These great seas of sand may cover areas as large as 193,000 square miles (500,000 square kilometers). Deserts also are found in continental interiors far from the sea.

Wind power

Wind is the most powerful force that shapes the desert. It picks up sand grains and transports them across the desert floor. The largest features of the desert shaped by the wind are called bedforms. Dunes and ripples develop on the bedforms as the wind moves the sand around. Where sand is deposited, dune crests tend to be arranged at right angles to the prevailing wind direction. Individual dunes have a steep front face and shallow back slope. Due to the way in which dunes grow, akin to the tipping of unwanted rock over the edge of a slag heap, bedforms are characterized by surfaces inclined to the horizontal, a characteristic called cross-bedding.

Dunes

In regions of fairly constant wind direction, widespread crescent-shaped dunes known as barchans form. Fields of such dunes often coalesce to produce a broad ripplelike swathe across the desert floor. On very bare rocky surfaces, the sand may be drawn out into

Cross-bedding

Inclined planes in sedimentary rocks caused by strong currents of water or wind during deposition.

Seif dunes

elongated seif dunes, whereas in regions of changeable wind direction, dunes with star-shaped structures develop.

Erosion

Erosion is another effect of the wind. The constant abrasion of particles in the air tends to result in well-rounded grains, more spherical than those that develop in river and marine environments. Larger fragments that the wind is unable to pick up may simply be dragged along the ground, generating faceted pebbles called dreikanter. Sand removal by the wind may create areas such as the 186-mile (300-km)-long Qattara basin in Libya, 440 feet (134 meters) below sea level. Erosion on the face of individual

Dreikanter

A faceted pebble sculpted by the activity of wind in a desert environment. Such pebbles are generated because they are too heavy to be lifted by the wind and are merely moved back and forth along the desert floor.

Dune formation

Dunes occur in four variations. Tail dunes are created by small obstacles such as bushes or hills blocking the wind. Crescent-shaped barchan dunes form in regions of regular wind direction and limited sand. They may migrate downwind at rates of up to 80 feet (25 meters) per year. Star dunes form where variable winds prevent regular deposition on any one face. Where winds are constantly shifting and there is a large supply of sand, seif dunes form. In the Sahara they reach 980 feet (300 meters) high and 186 miles (300 kilometers) long.

Tail dunes

Barchans

Star dunes

rocks—both small and large—produces strikingly different features, such as honeycombed cliff faces, rock arches, or pedestals.

Rain occasionally falls in even the driest deserts, usually during short but violent storms. When these occur, there may be rapid erosion and movement of material over very short periods. In this way, fluvial valleys and wadis form. Seasonal lakes, called playa, often occupy desert interiors. These are collecting grounds for finer-grained deposits.

Desert interiors may be rather flat, but they often have peripheral plateaus and isolated hills. The rocky plateaus within the desert are attacked by wind, and generate large deposits of fragmented bedrock of talus formed from blocks, and pebble-sized fragments, which accumulate at the feet of escarpments. These are too coarse to be moved by the wind, although the wind may blow finer sand into the spaces between the talus material.

Wadi

A steep-sided valley in a desert region temporarily occupied by an ephemeral stream.

Glaciers and Ice

Ice covers about 6 million square miles (15 million square kilometers) of the Earth's surface today—that is, about 0.003 percent. During the last Ice Age, ice sheets extended over large areas of North America and Europe. The Earth has active valley glaciers as well as polar ice sheets that retreat and advance with the seasons.

In these once glaciated regions, ice is now restricted to glaciers in the higher mountains. Evidence of their former extent is found in the glacial striations produced on rock surfaces by the scouring action of stones trapped at the base of moving ice sheets, and by the plucked form of rock outcrops, which now are known as roches moutonées.

Then as now, glaciers advanced and retreated along valleys in response to changes in climate. As they advanced, the glaciers carried debris scoured from the land; when they retreated, this debris was left as terminal moraines. The location of these deposits has allowed geologists to trace the various phases of the glaciation. The valleys themselves deepened and became steep at their sides, generating flat-bottomed, steep-sided, U-shaped profiles—a typical feature of glacial erosion.

Curriculum Context

The student is expected to know that water contributes to two processes that help shape the landscape—the breakdown of rock into smaller pieces by mechanical and chemical weathering, and the removal of rock and soil by erosion.

Milford Sound on the west coast of South Island, New Zealand, is a U-shaped valley that was carved out by ice-age glaciers as they moved slowly toward the sea. Now it is flooded by the sea to depths of over 1,680 feet (510 meters).

Glacial

A period of relative cold and consequent ice advance duing an ice age. Glacial periods are interspersed with interglacials, periods in which the climate becomes warmer and there is ice retreat.

Glacial landforms

The glaciers are still in retreat, and it is possible to see the depositional landforms that are their legacy. These include low, hummocky hills called drumlins and long, winding gravel ridges called eskers. Both are aligned parallel to the direction of ice movement, and the pattern of their ancient counterparts may be used to trace earlier glacial geography. In addition, at the sides of a typical valley glacier, coarse debris accumulates and forms lateral moraines.

The Upper Regions of a Glacier

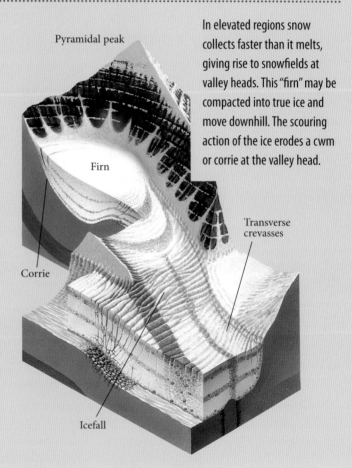

Pyramidal peak

Firn

Corrie

Transverse crevasses

Icefall

The debris carried by glaciers forms moraine. Some is carried along the margins, some at the moving glacier front, and some beneath the glacier. When the ice encounters irregularities, crevasses form, tending to lie at right angles to the flow. The toe of a glacier is characterized by meltwater ponds, seasonal streams, and terminal moraine debris.

In elevated regions snow collects faster than it melts, giving rise to snowfields at valley heads. This "firn" may be compacted into true ice and move downhill. The scouring action of the ice erodes a cwm or corrie at the valley head.

Although such features give vital clues to geologists, they do not form the bulk of glacial deposits. These are boulder clay, also known as "till", which is the morainic debris that accumulates beneath the ice. Within such debris may be blocks that have been transported from distant locations as well as a mixture of sand and gravel. Erratics left behind in lowland Britain after the retreat of the Pleistocene ice sheet include rocks as diverse as igneous rocks from Norway and chalk from East Anglia. Boulder clays that become compacted by

Boulder clay

A mixture of rock and finely pulverized rock flour that formed when it was dragged along at the base of a moving glacier and then left behind after the ice had melted.

Retreating Ice

The retreat of ice may leave a valley glacier above the main valley floor. The melting of ice reveals tear-shaped morainic mounds called drumlins, aligned in the original flow direction. Rock outcrops may be smoothed on one side and plucked on the other, forming roches moutonnées. Meltwater issuing from the glacier toe has the capacity of cutting down into both the subglacial moraine and the hanging valley floor.

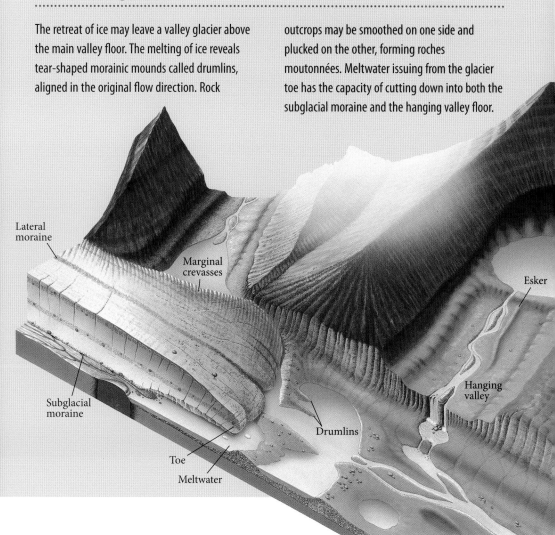

Lateral moraine

Marginal crevasses

Esker

Subglacial moraine

Hanging valley

Drumlins

Toe

Meltwater

burial are known as tillites. Identification of such rocks within the rock record has enabled geologists to show that glaciations occurred in the distant past in locations as unlikely as Australia, South America, and Africa.

Permafrost

Beyond the margins of any ice sheet the ground is still very cold—indeed, frozen. Regions of permafrost, as this ground is known, may thaw in summer. Such alternate freeze-thaw cycles heave up the ground surface and sort the different-sized fragments into mounds, forming patterned ground and giving rise on flat surfaces to stone polygons. Collapse depressions may form where ice mounds up beneath the surface during winter and then melts during the summer months, causing collapse. Elsewhere, ice-filled blisters pushed up by pressure from below may form pingos.

An aerial photograph of the Arctic tundra. Tundra comes from the Finnish word *tunturi*, meaning treeless plain. It is noted for its frost-molded landscapes, extremely low temperatures through most of the year, little precipitation, poor nutrients, and short growing seasons.

Life on Earth

Since the Sun and its system of planets were formed, about 4.5 billion years ago, younger stars—and possibly other planetary systems—have been born. Equally, since the Earth first came into existence, other stars and any attendant planets will long since have reached the end of their active lives. Will this happen to the Solar System?

Our Sun is currently in "middle age." Although its supply of hydrogen is abundant, eventually it will run low; this will probably occur about 5 billion years from now. Energy production will then cease, and the helium-rich core will begin to shrink under the influence of gravity. In doing so it will heat up again; and, because there will still be some hydrogen left around the core region, it will start reacting once more. The inert helium core will become surrounded by an envelope of burning hydrogen.

At this stage the Sun will begin to expand, while its helium core is still contracting. The helium will be converted to heavier elements such as oxygen and carbon, and energy will be dissipated into space, lowering the Sun's temperature. By the time it has dropped to about 3000°K (about half its present temperature), the Sun will be too cool to warm the Solar System. The Earth and other planets will not survive this stage. This will be the end of our world.

Three conditions appear to be necessary for life as it exists on Earth: no free hydrogen in the atmosphere; an ample supply of water; and the presence of hydrocarbons. These conditions do not exist on the other planets, and they have not always existed on Earth either.

Curriculum Context

Students should know the evidence from Earth and Moon rocks indicates that the Solar System was formed from a nebular cloud of dust and gas approximately 4.5 billion years ago.

Hydrocarbon

An organic chemical compound consisting predominantly of hydrogen and carbon. Coal, oil, and natural gas are three commonly occurring hydrocarbons.

Curriculum Context

Students should know that the Sun is a typical star and is powered by nuclear reactions, primarily the fusion of hydrogen to form helium.

Early atmosphere

Early in the history of the Earth, the planet's surface was not sufficiently shielded from harmful solar radiation to allow life to begin. The atmosphere was made primarily of nitrogen and carbon dioxide, and any water vapor was quickly split into hydrogen and oxygen by the effects of solar radiation. The hydrogen escaped into space, but oxygen reacted to form ozone (O_3) or remained as atomic oxygen (O). The ozone collected in the upper atmosphere to form a protective layer which shielded the surface from strong ultraviolet radiation, though this process must have taken a very long time.

Small amounts of metal–carbon compounds, or carbides, probably also existed, although not abundantly; their presence is suggested by the fact that such compounds are found in meteorites. When carbides react with water they form hydrocarbons. Though the early Earth did not contain a great deal of methane (CH_4), the little that existed may have provided hydrocarbon molecules too.

Guanine and thymine are two of the four bases in DNA, the molecule found in all living beings that encodes instructions for replication, and for the creation of a small number of amino acids, including glutamic acid, which can combine into complex molecules that form the structures of living organisms.

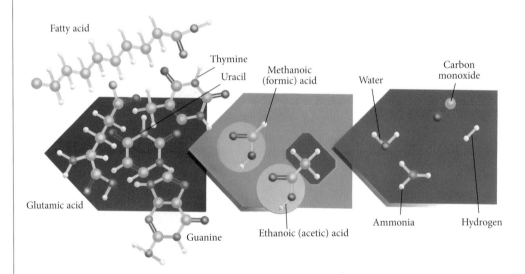

Fatty acid

Thymine

Uracil

Methanoic (formic) acid

Water

Carbon monoxide

Glutamic acid

Guanine

Ethanoic (acetic) acid

Ammonia

Hydrogen

Early life-forms

Life probably began either beneath the sea or in damp sheltered places near to it. Blue-green algae were among the first types of life to evolve.

By about 2.5 billion years ago, prokaryotes (simple marine organisms whose cells have no differentiated nucleus) evolved the capacity to use sunlight to make food: photosynthesis had begun. The prokaryotic cells gradually became more complex until, about 1.2 billion years ago, eukaryotes—organisms with a nucleus in each cell—appeared. Eukaryotes gave rise to the diverse life that now exists on our planet.

Eukaryote
A living cell that has a nucleus. Eukaryotes first appeared about 1.2 billion years ago.

In photosynthesis, a living cell (usually in a plant) takes in carbon dioxide and water, and gives off oxygen as an end product. Once photosynthesis had begun, the production of free oxygen (O_2) rose dramatically, and conditions became much more favorable for life. Early marine invertebrates had developed by the Cambrian period, but it was not until the close of the Devonian period 360 million years ago (during the early part of which fish had emerged onto land) that land-based life began to flourish. By the Permian period (286 million years ago), amphibians had evolved the capacity to lay hard-skinned amniotic (water-retaining) eggs; the first reptiles had evolved. Some evolved into dinosaurs, others into mammals.

Humans' direct ancestors were small, apelike hominids. The oldest known ancestor bones, from East Africa, are 4.5 million years old. By around 1.5 million years ago, upright humans (*Homo erectus*) developed the facility to use stone tools; about 50,000 years later, the making of fire had been accomplished. Half a million years ago, upright humans had spread into Europe and the Far East and were successful hunters as well as toolmakers. The rest is history.

The Gaia Hypothesis

The Gaia hypothesis is an extraordinary concept, easily dismissed at first, but with more careful analysis proves to be worthy of much greater investigation, if not widescale acceptance. Gaia was the Greek goddess of the Earth. The hypothesis states that the Earth, as a whole, should be viewed as a living organism.

Curriculum Context

Students should know how Earth's climate has changed over time, corresponding to changes in Earth's geography, atmospheric composition, and other factors, such as solar radiation and plate movements.

British scientist James Lovelock first proposed the idea during the 1960s. He was struck by the fact that the Earth's atmosphere betrays the fact that Earth is inhabited. The metabolism of living creatures on Earth drives the composition of the atmosphere out of chemical equilibrium. In other words, chemicals such as methane and oxygen, which would not normally be expected to coexist with one another, are produced by organisms and are present in large quantities in the Earth's atmosphere. None of the other planets in the Solar System contains such an unlikely mix of chemicals in their atmospheres.

If life is altering the composition of the atmosphere to this extent, perhaps it is helping shape other parts of the world, too. Perhaps the various species and life forms on this world are analogous to the individual living cells within us. Each is alive and all interact in such a way that they unconsciously give rise to an even larger organism.

Lovelock likens the idea of the Earth to that of a giant redwood tree. While the tree is undoubtedly alive, 99 percent of its makeup is dead. The interior is made of lignin and cellulose, while the only living cells are contained in the bark—the thin outer layer of the tree. Thus the Earth, mostly made of rocks and other inanimate material, can be thought of as a single, living metaorganism because of the small percentage of living matter on its surface.

Certainly the life forms on Earth have the ability to alter the global condition of the planet. For example, carbon dioxide can be scrubbed from the atmosphere by the metabolism of oceanic algae. Also, not only the atmosphere is affected by life forms. Lovelock cites certain properties of the rocks and waters of the planet, such as temperature, oxidation, and acidity, which are all kept within defined limits by the daily activities of living things. Thus, the conditions are self-perpetuating.

Where humankind fits into this scheme is difficult to interpret. The working of Gaia appears to rely on the unconscious interaction of the planet's lifeforms. Humans, however, are conscious. Through the development of science, technology, and industry, we have developed the capacity to affect the environment to an extent never before experienced by Gaia, except in times of extreme crisis such as ice ages and following asteroid impacts. Industrial pollution and the widescale use of fossil fuels and mineral reserves all place our world under stress. Shifting weather patterns and climate change could be Gaia's first response to these disruptive factors.

Many scientists and other people believe that the governments of the industrial nations must place conservation and ecology high on their list of priorities. If the human race is going to continue to live and prosper, they believe that new ways of working sympathetically with the environment, instead of against it, must be found. Utilizing natural power sources such as solar energy, wind, and tidal power is not easy but must increasingly become a part of our lives.

Curriculum Context

The student is expected to analyze conditions on Earth that enable organisms to survive.

Natural Catastrophes

In Armero, Colombia, South America, there was a sequence of earthquakes during November 1984. Steam emissions increased one month later; then, on September 11, 1985, a small explosion threw ash and rocks—parts of the old crater of Nevada del Ruiz volcano—into the air. Nobody appeared to be particularly worried, despite the fact that local officials had been warned that the town of Armero was built on top of a mudflow that had covered the region in 1845, killing 1000 people. The risk was clear, but nothing was done.

Two days later, 22,000 people in the area were dead. A relatively small eruption had ejected a blanket of hot pumice and ash that melted snowfields high on the volcano above. The meltwater rushed downhill at speeds of more than 22 mph (35 km/h), gathering soil, rocks, and trees as it did so, and generated a devastating mudflow which raced through the town in a wall 100 feet (30 meters) high. This spread out over the lowlying ground as a series of hot waves, carrying blocks as large as 33 feet (10 meters) high with it. At its peak, an estimated 62,000 cubic yards (47,000 cubic meters) per second of debris sped downhill: roughly one fifth the discharge rate of the mighty Amazon River.

Predicting disasters

Natural disasters on this scale are rare; nevertheless, they do happen. Ironically, the scale of the disaster caused by the mudflow in Colombia could at least have been lessened. Predicting the behavior of volcanoes has become a serious business, largely in the wake of the eruptions of Mount St. Helens and El Chichon in the early 1980s. In 1991, lessons learned from these events were successfully applied to the massive eruption of Mount Pinatubo in the Philippines, so that mass evacuation of inhabitants of the surrounding regions

Volcanoes are one of the most spectacular natural catastrophes. Thick clouds of ash tower as high as 12 miles (20 kilometers) into the air. The ash may be deposited on the ground to a depth of 6 inches (15 centimeters). Within a few miles of the blast site, everything is destroyed; the ash will often carry for several hundred miles and disrupt weather systems all over the globe.

could be accomplished before the ash descended, forming a 6-inch- (15-centimeter-) thick layer.

Earthquakes

Earthquakes too have caused large-scale loss of life and widespread damage to property and communications. San Francisco and neighboring settlements that lie along the San Andreas Fault in California are particularly at risk. In 1989 this fault ruptured, reactivating older fractures that had been opened as long ago as 1906. The quake, which registered 7.1 on the Richter Scale, claimed 62 lives and destroyed nearly 1,000 homes. In January 1994 a quake on an associated fault caused a similar degree of damage in Los Angeles. This region is one of the most closely monitored seismic zones on Earth. Although the local and state authorities can do nothing to avert an earthquake, their catastrophic

Earthquake

The sudden movement of rocks along a deep-seated fault plane, which sets off seismic waves generated by the abrupt release of potential energy inside the Earth. It is the resultant vibrations that are felt as earthquakes.

effects can be lessened by enforcing strict regulations about building structures. The death toll from earthquakes elsewhere in the world indicates how much this matters: a quake of similar strength killed 20,000 in China in 1974.

Ancient impact

There is evidence of one natural disaster that had possible global significance. In recent years, it has been proposed that the extinction of the dinosaurs about 65 million years ago resulted from an enormous impact—possibly from a meteorite 6 miles (10 kilometers) in diameter striking the Earth, raising its temperature and causing darkness for several weeks. This is known as the K/T boundary event from the evidence which comes from a layer of rock at the Cretaceous–Tertiary boundary. Within it are higher than average amounts of iridium, believed to be derived from the meteorite; widespread shocked quartz, feldspar, and stishovite (formed at very high pressures); remains of soot (possibly from forest fires caused by the impact); and anomalously high ratios of strontium isotopes, the result of increased weathering rates due to nitric acid rain formed from atmospheric nitrogen during the impact.

This event (or some other natural disaster) set the stage for mammalian evolution to proceed. It eventually allowed *Homo sapiens* to proliferate without competition from the highly successful predecessors that had ruled the world for millions of years.

K/T boundary

K is the traditional abbreviation for the Cretaceous period, and T is the abbreviation for the Tertiary period. The K/T boundary marks the end of the Mesozoic era, and the beginning of the Cenozoic era.

Global Climate

The Earth is the only known planet to support life. The first organisms appeared more than 3.5 billion years ago; today there are millions of species inhabiting the biosphere—the part of the planet where life is found. Climate is among the most influential factors that determine their survival.

The Earth relies on a constant supply of light and heat energy produced by the Sun, which is absorbed both by Earth's atmosphere and by the land and oceans below. The amount of heat that reaches the surface varies, creating climatic zones: tropical, temperate, and polar.

The climatic zones are linked to areas of high and low atmospheric pressure. When air near the ground is heated, it expands and becomes less dense, creating an area of low pressure. The warm air rises, while cool air flows in to replace it. The result is a convection current of circulating air. The rising warm air cools as it gets higher in the atmosphere and increases in

Buffalo assemble at a watering hole in Kenya. Kenya has a hot, tropical climate. The vegetation seen here is savanna grassland, with scattered trees and shrubs. Summers are hot and very dry. Almost all of the rain falls during the winter. Animals migrate every year in search of food.

Climate

The characteristic weather conditions of a particular place over a period of time. It encompasses meteorological elements and the factors that influence them.

Curriculum Context

The student is expected to describe the transfer of heat energy at the boundaries between the atmosphere, land masses, and oceans resulting in layers of different temperatures and densities in both the ocean and atmosphere.

density. It begins to sink back down, forming a high-pressure area. Global temperature differences cause a circulation of air currents, with warm air rising from the tropics and moving toward the Poles, distributing heat energy along the way. In general, there are areas of low pressure over the Equator and the temperate regions; high-pressure areas cover the polar regions and the semitropical regions immediately north and south of the Equator.

Energy Distribution over the Earth

At the Equator, the Sun is overhead for much of the year and its rays strike the ground almost vertically. Little heat is lost as the rays pass through the atmosphere so most reaches the ground. The poles receive much less energy because the Sun is low in the sky for much of the year and the rays have a lot of atmosphere to pass through. The movement of air transfers the heat from the Equator toward the poles. Warm air rises over the Equator, producing a belt of low pressure, and sinks over the subtropics as hot, dry air. Some of this air flows back toward the Equator, forming the trade winds, and some flows away from it. Cold air subsiding over the poles flows outward as easterly winds until it meets tropical air flowing toward the poles. The two types of air then rise side by side. The polar air flows toward the poles and the tropical air flows toward the Equator.

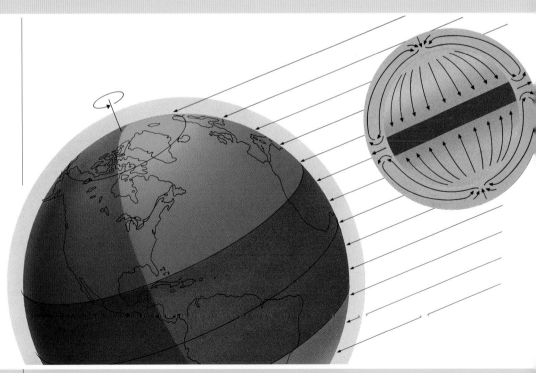

The uneven distribution of rainfall is another important aspect of the different climatic zones, and it depends on both temperature and air movements. Tropical regions receive the greatest amount of incoming heat energy from the Sun, which evaporates huge amounts of water from the oceans and (to a lesser extent) the land. Warm air can hold more moisture than cool air, which tends to be dry—the warm air has a higher humidity.

As the tropical air rises, it cools and loses moisture, much of which falls back on the tropics as rain. The cooler, drier air then continues moving north and south, depositing little moisture in the warm temperate zone. As it passes over the warm land, it is warmed again, and more moisture is released in the cool temperate zone. By the time the air reaches the Poles, it is dry and cold.

Climate determines what vegetation can grow in a region, and how much. Tropical regions receive the most heat and moisture, and have the highest productivity—the total vegetation grown, usually measured in kilograms per square meter (kg/m^2). Rainforest produces about 3.5 kg/m^2 per year, compared with less than 0.1 kg/m^2 in deserts and polar regions. Productivity in deserts is limited by lack of water and in polar regions by lack of heat and light.

Tropical climate
Describing the climate typical of the tropics, an area lying between the Tropics of Cancer and Capricorn. These two latitudes are the limits of the Earth's surface in which the Sun can be directly overhead.

Recent Climate Change

About 2.4 million years ago, the climate began to grow colder all over the world. Snow that fell in winter lay for longer in spring and the area covered by snow throughout the year slowly increased. As more snow fell, its weight compressed the snow at the base until it turned into solid ice.

The ice advanced until it covered all of Canada and the United States roughly to a line from Seattle to New York, and most of Europe north of a line from London to Berlin and Moscow. The ice grew thicker each year until eventually the vast ice sheets were more than one mile (1.6 kilometers) thick in some places. The Earth had entered an ice age.

This was not the first ice age. They have happened occasionally over the last billion or so years of the Earth's history. But the one that began about 2.4 million years ago was the first of a series of ice ages that probably is still continuing today. During this time, each ice age has lasted for approximately 40,000–100,000 years and ice ages have been separated by warmer intervals, called interglacials, each lasting for about 10,000–30,000 years.

The Wisconsinan

The most recent ice age is called the Wisconsinan in North America. It began about 75,000 years ago and ended about 10,000 years ago. Wisconsinan is its American name, but the ice sheets also covered Europe at roughly the same time. The ice age is known as the Devensian in Britain, Weichselian in northern Europe, and Würm in the Alps. During this ice age the average temperature was about 6°C (11°F) lower than it is today.

About 21,000 years ago, the ice sheets reached their greatest extent. This period is known as the "last glacial

Curriculum Context

Students should know how Earth's climate has changed over time, corresponding to changes in Earth's geography, atmospheric composition, and other factors, such as solar radiation and plate movement.

maximum." Over the ice, the temperature would have risen above freezing for a very short time during the summer, but then rapidly plunged deep below freezing during the rest of the year. The eastern North Atlantic Ocean was covered with ice as far south as central Portugal, but with a gap between this ice and the ice extending along the North American coast as far as New York.

The climate was very dry. Very little water evaporates into cold air, so clouds cannot form. The sky was clear blue, except when the constant winds blew powdery snow from the surface of the ice and produced the whiteout of a fierce blizzard. When it did snow, the snow remained where it fell. Over the centuries, more and more snow accumulated on the ice sheets. The snow consisted of water that had evaporated from the lakes and oceans and its steady removal over the centuries caused the sea level to fall by 300–425 feet (90–130 meters).

Retreat of ice
Then, as the Earth moved out of the last glacial maximum, the weather grew warmer. Sometimes the falling snow turned to rain. By 15,000 years ago the ice sheet over the western coast of Europe was melting rapidly and in North America ice had gone from the basins that formed the Great Lakes. Around 13,000 years ago a passage opened from the Great Lakes— which were by then filling with water—through the Saint Lawrence River and into the Atlantic Ocean. As the huge Laurentian ice sheet covering Québec melted, its water flowed directly into the North Atlantic. By 8,500 years ago the ice had retreated from all of Europe apart from the mountains of northern Scandinavia. In North America, the Laurentian ice sheet still covered northeastern Canada and the Keewatin ice sheet covered most of the area to the west of Hudson Bay.

In some places the climate changed very rapidly. It took longer for the huge sheets of ice to melt, but the average global temperature could change from that of a full ice age to that of today—or even warmer—in as little as three years. As the ice melted, the sea level rose, sometimes very fast indeed. When lakes at the edge of the ice began discharging water into the Arctic Ocean about 8,500 years ago, the sea level all over the world rose 8–16 inches (20–40 centimeters) in a few days. At various other times the seas rose by more than 1½ inches (4.5 centimeters) a year and continued doing so for more than a century.

Life returns

As the temperature rose and the ice retreated, the ground began to thaw and rivers of cold, clean water began to flow. Plant seeds and the spores of ferns and fungi, carried by the wind, settled on the moist ground and sprouted. Birds venturing from warmer latitudes in search of food and nesting sites dropped more seeds. Seals flopped ashore. Insects arrived, as did spiders ballooning on their long silken threads. It was not long before plants were growing across the newly exposed land, insects were feeding on them and pollinating them, spiders were hunting the insects, and there were birds and, later, land mammals. The world was returning to life after its long winter.

Then, about 11,000 years ago, it all went wrong. Water from the Laurentian ice sheet was flooding into the North Atlantic. The edge of the sea ice retreated to a line from Iceland to Newfoundland. Both events released fresh water that floated on top of the salt sea water. Its effect was to alter the pattern of ocean currents that normally transport warm water northward from the equator. The temperature at the ocean surface dropped by 13–18°F (7–10°C) and the sea ice re-advanced to about the latitude of Montréal. Air crossing the ocean was chilled by contact with the

A glacier winds its way through the mountains of Greenland. The world is now in a comparatively warm interglacial period (that we call the Flandrian) but is expected eventually to become colder as another ice age approaches. However, this pattern may be disturbed if recent temperature trends do actually indicate that global warming is taking place.

water. Temperatures in Europe fell to those of the ice age, the ice sheets returned to the western Highlands of Scotland, and the cold episode lasted for about 1,000 years. Scientists first learned of this cold period when they found pollen from an alpine plant, mountain avens, in soils where the climate is now too warm for it to grow naturally. The Latin name for this plant is *Dryas octopetala* and so the cold period is known as the Dryas. In fact, it is called the Younger Dryas, because a similar cold spell occurred earlier, from about 12,200 through 11,800 years ago.

The ice age finally ended about 10,000 years ago and the world entered a new interglacial, called the Flandrian. We are still living in the Flandrian.

Weather Patterns

The daily pattern of conditions such as temperature and rainfall is called weather. It may change from day to day or even from hour to hour. Climate is based on the average weather conditions over a long period—about 30 years—and changes very slowly.

Curriculum Context

Students should know that weather (in the short run) and climate (in the long run) involve the transfer of energy into and out of the atmosphere.

Weather begins with air movements. Warm air is less dense than cold air, so it tends to rise (convect), causing a reduction in atmospheric pressure. Wind blows from high-pressure to low-pressure areas. If the Earth did not rotate, cold, high-pressure air would simply flow from the Poles toward the Equator, while warm, low-pressure air from the Equator flowed toward the Poles. However, convection currents in the atmosphere are affected by the spin of the Earth on its axis. The warm, rising air spins more slowly than the Earth. Because of this, it moves along a curved path. In the northern hemisphere it is deflected to the right, and in the southern hemisphere it is deflected to the left. This is called the Coriolis effect. It also influences the direction of high-pressure systems (anticyclones) and low-pressure systems (cyclones). Anticyclones are

The Coriolis effect, caused by the Earth's rotation on its axis, deflects winds to the right in the northern hemisphere and to the left in the southern hemisphere. This complicates the basic pattern of warm air flowing north and cool air flowing south.

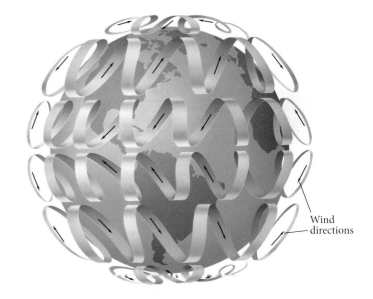

Wind directions

associated with calm weather, cyclones with disturbances such as tropical storms.

The Doldrums

At the Equator is a region of calm, warm, low-pressure air called the Doldrums. When it rises, it causes streams of high-pressure air to move toward the Equator from the north and south to replace it. These high-pressure streams are the trade winds. They do not blow directly north and south, for they are influenced by the Coriolis effect. The trade winds span nearly half the globe and dominate the weather systems of the tropics and semi-tropics.

Next to the zone of the trade winds, between about 30° and 60° latitude (the temperate zone), are the westerlies, the second major global wind system. Westerlies blow toward the Poles and are particularly strong in the southern hemisphere, where there is less large land mass to lessen their force. In the temperate zone, cold air from the Poles (called easterlies) meets the warm air from the tropics. These do not mix easily. The interaction of cold and warm currents and the

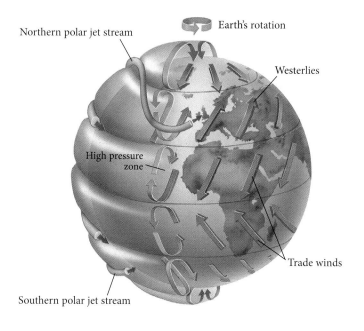

Northern polar jet stream

Earth's rotation

Westerlies

High pressure zone

Trade winds

Southern polar jet stream

Hot air rises at the Equator, cooling and sinking over the tropics to create high-pressure zones. Some is drawn back to the Equator, forming the trade winds; the rest moves toward the poles.

spinning of the Earth result in high, fast-moving winds called jet streams. They are found 5-6 miles (8–10 kilometers) above the surface of the Earth, traveling at 125 mph (200 km/h). A jet stream is rather like a snaking tube that weaves an unsteady path, creating a series of areas of low and high pressure.

Shifting winds

Unlike the Doldrums, which are a permanent fixture at the Equator, the large belts of winds—the trade winds and the jet stream—shift with the changing seasons as the Earth heats up and cools down. This is one of the chief factors that produce weather conditions. For example, when the jet stream moves north, the air beneath becomes less dense and the tropical warm air can move north too, creating an area of low pressure. If it drifts to the south, denser, cold air moves south, creating a high-pressure area. The changing patterns of low- and high-pressure areas give countries in the temperate zones their changeable weather patterns. In the northern hemisphere, hot, sunny weather results when the jet stream moves north in summer, allowing warm tropical air to cover the land. When the jet stream moves south in winter, cold polar air moves south too, bringing cold winds and clear skies. Long-range weather forecasts attempt to predict the path of the jet streams because they have such a significant influence on the weather.

The trade winds move north and south over the Equator by about 5°—except over India, where they move by as much as 30°. This is partly due to the high temperature of the continent, which warms the air and creates low-pressure zones. These conditions are reinforced by shifts in the local jet stream, which moves to the south in the winter, bringing dry, high-pressure air down to India from the Tibetan plateau; in the summer it recedes back to the north, and the local low-pressure system resumes.

Moving Oceans

More than 70 percent of the Earth's surface is covered by water, nearly all of which is in the oceans. The oceans were created millions of years ago when the Earth was relatively young. The cooling planet was surrounded by a layer of gases which included water vapor. Gravity prevented these gases from escaping into space.

As the Earth cooled, its atmosphere could not hold all the water vapor; much of it condensed to form the five oceans: the Atlantic, Pacific, Indian, Arctic, and Antarctic (also called the Southern Ocean). In parts of the Pacific Ocean, the water is more than 7 miles (11 kilometers) deep.

The oceans play a number of important roles in the biosphere. They act as a huge "sink" (absorber) for atmospheric carbon dioxide, much of which is incorporated in the skeletons of marine animals. They help to regulate the global climate by moving warm water from the Equator toward the Poles, and cold water from the Poles toward the Equator. Oceans are also the primary component of the water cycle, supplying huge amounts of water to the atmosphere to be distributed over the Earth as rain.

Convection currents

The water in the oceans is never still, because the oceans contain water currents much like the airflow in the atmosphere. Currents are produced by the effects of wind and by convection—the upward movement of warm water. The Sun over the Equator causes tropical waters to increase in temperature. Warm water is less dense than cold water, so it rises, causing convection currents. In the southern hemisphere, the warm currents move south to the temperate regions.

Ocean

Any great mass of salt water. There are five oceans on Earth and together they cover almost 70 percent of the total surface area of the Earth. Oceans are complex biomes and play a major role in the water cycle, as well as shaping the climates of different regions.

Ocean Currents

The Gulf Stream (top center), the Brazil current (bottom center), the Kuroshio current off Japan (top left), and the Agulhas current off southern Africa (bottom right), are all warm currents, shown in red. Continents force the water to circulate within each ocean. Warm currents tend to form fast-flowing narrow bands and flow poleward on the western side of the ocean; cold currents are broad and slow. Deep-water currents move toward the Equator from the Poles, rising to the surface and joining the circulation.

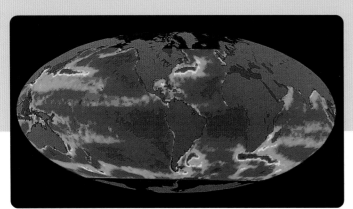

The opposite happens in the north; the warm currents move north toward the Pole. As the water cools, it sinks and moves back toward the Equator. These warm currents have a considerable effect on local climates. The Gulf Stream, the current that moves north from the Caribbean across the Atlantic to northern Europe, creates mild winters in Europe. Similar warm currents are important to areas of northern Japan and Alaska, where the climate would be much more severe in winter if not for a warm offshore current.

Cold currents

There are also cold currents that move toward the Equator from the polar regions. Cold currents, upwelling from deep seas, are rich in

Winds create surface currents, which are deflected by the Coriolis effect so that the water moves at a 45° angle to the wind. A sailboat rides the current, pushed by the wind.

nutrients and support a rich and diverse community of plants and animals. An abundance of plankton attracts larger animals such as fish and whales. The Peru current, for example, flows up the eastern coast of South and North America. However, every 2 to 7 years the westward-flowing South Equatorial Current weakens and the stagnating warm water suppresses the cold upwellings. When this happens the resulting weather disturbance is called an El Niño.

Curriculum Context

The student is expected to describe the effects of phenomena such as El Niño and jet streams on local weather.

Surface winds cause waves to form. The size of the waves depends on the area of open water and the strength of the winds. Together, waves and tidal rhythms influence the shoreline communities.

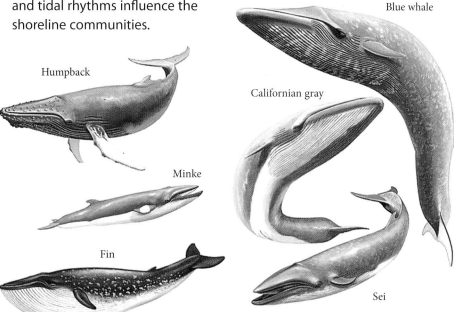

Blue whale

Humpback

Californian gray

Minke

Fin

Sei

Whales

Whales are marine mammals that travel the world, following the plankton and fish on which they feed. Baleen whales are the biggest animals on Earth. The blue whale feeds in the Southern Ocean during the summer and moves into the tropics for the winter. Humpback and fin whales live in both hemispheres, as does the sei, but the latter does not visit the polar regions.

Seasonal Changes

As the Earth orbits the Sun, it is tilted at an angle of 23.5° on an axis that joins the North and South Poles. Only one part of the Earth faces the Sun as it spins. This causes the phenomenon of night and day at different times across the globe.

Seasonal and daily changes are also governed by the way in which the Earth orbits the Sun. Most significantly, this affects the weather patterns of the temperate zones north and south of the tropics. For six months of the year, from May to September, the northern end of the Earth's axis is pointed toward the Sun. As the alignment of the axis approaches the Sun, the Sun appears higher in the sky in the northern hemisphere, allowing more heat and light energy to reach the land, and increasing the temperature. On the summer solstice, the Sun reaches its highest angle, and the daylight lasts longest. For the other six months, from October to April, the southern hemisphere is tilted at the Sun. While the southern hemisphere experiences its summer, the northern hemisphere undergoes winter. As the Sun gets progressively lower in the sky, and less heat and light reach the ground, the days become shorter and colder.

The tilt of the Earth as it orbits the Sun causes seasons in the higher latitudes. New seasons are marked by two equinoxes each year when night (2) and day (4) are of equal length; and two solstices, one the longest day (1) and the other the shortest day (3).

Tropical daylength

In the tropics—which lie within 23.5° on either side of the Equator—the Sun is always relatively high in the sky. There is little seasonal variation in temperature and the air remains warm all year. Daylength remains almost constant throughout the year, with 12 hours of daylight and 12 hours of darkness. In the regions bordering the tropics, there are often distinct dry and wet seasons, though the temperature remains warm.

The Arctic and Antarctic are always very cold. In summer, the Sun never sets at the Poles, and there is continuous daylight. These few months are the warmest. In the middle of winter, the Sun never rises above the horizon and there is continuous night. One of the most dramatic seasonal changes occurs during the Antarctic winter. During the cold winter months, the size of the continent is doubled by the formation of sea ice, in some places extending more than 620 miles (1000 kilometers) from the land mass.

Seasonal winds

There are a number of seasonal winds. The mistral is a cold northerly wind that blows in the Mediterranean region during the winter months. Several hot dry winds blow from the Sahara throughout the same region between March and June. In North America, a warm dry wind blows down the eastern side of the Rocky Mountains in early spring. Called the chinook ("snow eater"), it causes a rapid melting of the snow. Many semitropical areas, particularly in southeast Asia, are affected by monsoon winds, which bring heavy rains in the summer but dry air in the winter.

Animals and plants have to adapt to these seasonal changes in order to survive. The change in day length, called the photo period, often provides the stimulus to change a pattern of behavior. Many birds migrate between regions of the world at different times of year

Monsoon
A seasonal wind pattern that brings heavy rain to southern Asia. It blows from the northeast (toward the sea) in winter and rain-laden from the southwest (toward the land) in summer. The monsoon cycle is believed to have started about 12 million years ago with the uplift of the Himalayas.

in order to maintain a good food supply. Barn swallows, for example, live in North America and Eurasia during the warm summer months. In the fall, as the days get shorter, they fly south to South America, South Asia, and Africa, returning the following spring.

Hibernation

A state of greatly reduced metabolism and suspended bodily activity by which some animals survive the winter months of food scarcity and cold weather.

Hibernation

Animals that cannot migrate often hibernate through the winter. They do this by reducing their heart rate and body temperature, and entering a resting phase during which they remain dormant through the winter months. The shortening days act as a trigger to prepare them for hibernation. They collect food and build up a store of body fat that must last them through the cold winter months. In the spring, many animals start their courtship rituals. Breeding in the spring ensures that their young are born in summer when there is plenty of food and they can fully develop before the arrival of winter.

White storks nest upon a power line support. Storks migrate annually from northern Europe to spend the northern winter in Africa or the Middle East. Animals that migrate seasonally navigate by a combination of magnetic sensing and ultrasound.

Plant adaptations

Plants, too, are affected by the length of the day. Some plants flower only when the days are long, thereby ensuring that their flowers are pollinated by the available insects. Others flower when the nights are long. However, in the tropics, where seasonal effects are minimal, plants flower throughout the year.

The World's Biomes

Life exists in only a small part of the Earth—in the lower atmosphere, on the surface, and in the oceans. Together these form a single large ecosystem called the biosphere. Within it, organisms may live on land or in the water. These two different environments may be divided further into biomes, which are characterized by the kinds of plants that grow there.

Land covers less than a third of the surface of the planet, but 90 percent of all species live on it. The characteristic plants of a biome support typical groups of animals. This distribution of life forms around the globe is far from random. It is closely linked to the climatic zones—polar, temperate, and tropical— because climate is a major factor that determines whether an animal or plant survives.

Temperature and rainfall

The two most important factors that influence which species can live in which land biome are the temperature and the amount of rainfall. These produce three main categories of terrestrial biome—grassland, forest, and desert—in each of the climate zones. A

Curriculum Context

The student is expected to analyze the range of atmospheric conditions that organisms will tolerate, including types of gases, temperature, particulate matter, and moisture.

Biomes are often similar on different continents: African grassland (left) looks very similar to that of South America or Australia (below).

forest, for example, may be cold (northern Canada), temperate (the Black Forest in central Europe), or tropical (the rainforest of central Africa).

Biomes do not have precise boundaries, but blend into one another across broad geographical regions. Their patterns vary with climate, so that parts of the North African desert are at the same latitude as the temperate forests of the southeastern United States. The detailed climate of an area depends, to a large extent, on the arrangement of land and sea. Because land masses warm up and cool down more rapidly than bodies of water, continental land masses experience quite different climates than do islands at

Terrestrial Biomes

Saltwater biomes cover most of the planet, but most life is found on land. A map of the continents shows how terrestrial biomes are distributed in a pattern corresponding to the climatic zones: polar, cool temperate, warm temperate, and tropical. Varying amounts of rain contribute to the differences between the main types of terrestrial biome: forest, grassland, and desert. The same type of biome may be found at different latitudes, and the same type of biome may be found in more than one climate. On a mountain, there may be a tropical biome at the base, forest on the slope, and a polar biome at the peak.

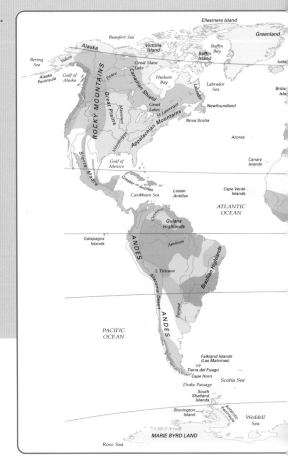

the same latitudes. Continental climates have cold winters and warm summers, whereas maritime climates, which are influenced by the ocean currents, often have milder winters but wetter summers.

Aquatic biomes

Climate is much less important in aquatic biomes. The single most important factor that determines what life can flourish in water is the amount of salt it contains. Salt-water aquatic biomes cover a much larger area of the Earth than any other biome, but they do not support as much life. Most marine life is found in the shallower water—down to about 650 feet (200 meters) in depth—over the continental shelves and slopes, where ultimately it depends on the abundance of plankton.

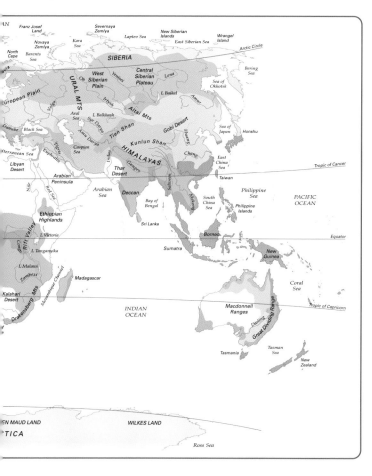

Maritime climate
A maritime climate is the climate typically found along many west coasts at middle latitudes and in southeast Australia.

On the Land

Land-based (terrestrial) biomes supply most of the world's food and have a major impact on the global climate—forests, for instance, play a crucial role in stabilizing the oxygen/carbon dioxide balance of the atmosphere. Varying temperatures and amounts of rainfall produce the patterns of vegetation that characterize the terrestrial biomes.

Curriculum Context

Students should know that rainforests and deserts on Earth are distributed in bands at specific latitudes.

Tropical rainforests grow in regions with strong sunlight, considerable rainfall, and warm temperatures year-round. This biome is the richest on Earth in the diversity of its plant and animal life—it has as many as half the Earth's species. The soil is surprisingly low in nutrients, which break down quickly in the hot, moist environment and are rapidly absorbed by plants.

Tropical rainforests have year-round hot weather and high rainfall. This biome supports a huge number of plant and animal species.

Polar biomes range from permanent ice and snow to tundra—frozen grassland that covers nearly 20 percent of the Earth's land area. Mosses, lichens, and other low-growing plants form a thick layer over the ground, which thaws slightly during the summer.

In the mid-latititudes of the temperate zone, coniferous forests of pine and spruce give way to deciduous broadleaf woodlands. Large plains stretch across the temperate zone, from the steppes of Eurasia to the pampas of South America.

In the warm temperate zone of the lower mid-latitudes, a drier climate has mixed grassland, warm evergreen forests, and aromatic shrubs; maquis and chaparral give way to desert.

Both water and heat are abundant in the tropical biomes of savanna (grassland) and rainforest, where plant and animal life are at their most diverse.

Temperate forests are found where there are distinct seasonal changes and moderate rainfall spread evenly over the seasons. Most of the trees are deciduous. Summer is the main growing season, while in the winter, plants are dormant. Temperate forest is less productive and diverse than tropical forest, but it is home to animal species from birds to large predators. Because their timber is valuable, little remains of the temperate forests that once covered much of Europe and North America.

Taiga

Boreal forest, or taiga, stretches across most of the world in a belt between the Arctic and temperate zones. The climate is cold, with long winters; water is plentiful, but frozen for much of the year. Because of the short growing season, boreal forest has little diversity of plant species, but these support a relatively large number of animals, from squirrels to grizzly bears. Insects and birds thrive in the short summers.

Savannas

Tropical grasslands, called savannas, grow in areas with warm year-round temperatures and plentiful rainfall. In addition to grasses, there may be small trees and shrubs. Most of the world's hoofed animals live in savannas, along with a wide range of other animal species. Temperate grasslands cover large regions in the interiors of continents. They include the prairies of North America and the pampas of South America, the veldt of southern Africa and the steppes of central Europe. The rich soil and variable but mild climate make these regions ideal for agriculture, and in many places the original grass has been cleared for farming or by grazing of livestock.

Tundra

Arctic grasslands, called tundra, are found at extreme northern latitudes but south of the polar ice at the

Arctic Circle. The vegetation is dominated by low-growing perennial plants able to survive the cold conditions, harsh winds, and dark winters. Temperatures range between –22°F (–30°C) in winter (which lasts six to ten months) and 50°F (10°C) in summer. Most precipitation falls as snow.

The tundra is highly productive during the brief three to four months of summer and supports a rich variety of wildlife. However, most animals migrate or hibernate long before the worst of the winter weather arrives.

Permafrost

Ground that is permanently frozen. It covers approximately 26 percent of the world's land surface in alpine areas and near glacial zones, and gives rise to a poorly drained form of grassland known as tundra.

Deserts

Deserts are areas that receive little rain, often less than 1 inch (25 millimeters) per year. Most are hot, and are found in tropical regions where air temperatures may rise to 122 °F (50°C) and surface temperatures to 194°F (90°C). Few plants can survive such arid conditions. There are also cold deserts such as the Gobi Desert in Mongolia and China. Parts of Antarctica, too, are technically deserts; one rocky valley has seen no moisture in any form for 200 years, making it the driest place on Earth.

Tundra topsoils are frozen for many months of the year, with only the surface thawing briefly in summer. The permanently frozen soil is called permafrost.

Glossary

Accretion The enlargement of a continent by the tectonic addition of other crustal fragments.

Archean The earliest part of Precambrian time, extending from the birth of the Earth as a planet to 2500 million years ago. Rocks of this age do not generally contain fossil remains.

Benioff zone The steeply inclined zone of seismic activity that extends downward from an oceanic trench toward the asthenosphere. Named for H. Benioff, a designer of musical instruments and seismographs, such zones mark the path of a tectonic plate being subducted at a destructive plate margin.

Benthic Describing the region at the bottom of a pond, lake, or ocean, and the animals that live there.

Boulder clay A mixture of rock and finely pulverized rock flour that formed when it was dragged along at the base of a moving glacier and then left behind after the ice had melted. Boulder clay is also known as till.

Continental Drift A theory, generally attributed to Alfred Wegener, postulating the early existence of a single ancient supercontinent that eventually broke up, beginning to drift apart about 200 million years ago.

Craton A region of ancient crust at the heart of a continent, which has evaded tectonic deformation for a protracted period.

Cross-bedding Inclined planes in sedimentary rocks caused by strong currents of water or wind during deposition.

Dreikanter A faceted pebble sculpted by the activity of wind in a desert environment. Such pebbles are generated because they are too heavy to be lifted by the wind and are merely moved back and forth along the desert floor.

Drumlin An elongated hillock composed of sediment deposited by a glacier, with its longer axis parallel to the direction of ice movement.

Eukaryote A living cell that has a nucleus. Eukaryotes first appeared about 1.2 billion years ago.

Eutrophic Describing freshwater habitats that are rich in plant nutrients. Such areas of water can give rise to shortlived algal blooms that may kill aquatic animals and higher plants

Feldspar The general name for a group of aluminosilicate rock-forming minerals that have an atomic structure in which a framework of oxygen atoms are shared by adjacent silicon atoms. They are of considerable importance and occur in a wide variety of rocks.

Gabbro A coarse-grained igneous rock that is chemically equivalent to basalt. Essential minerals found in gabbro are the calcium-rich plagioclase feldspar and pyroxesne, usually the variety augite.

Glacial A period of relative cold and consequent ice advance during an ice age. Glacial periods are interspersed with interglacials, periods in which the climate becomes warmer and there is ice retreat.

Graben A downfaulted block of crust bordered by a pair of normal faults, caused by extensional deformation. Graben formation is common on the crest and flanks of rising crustal domes, such as the Kenya Dome in East Africa.

Isostacy The principle that the rocks of the Earth's crust "float" on those of the underlying mantle.

Isotope One of a number of forms of an element that has the same number of protons in the nucleus but a different tally of neutrons (and therefore a different relative atomic mass).

Jet stream A 300-mile (483-km) wide channel of wind with an average speed of 65 mph (105 km/h) that occurs at altitudes of 6-10 miles (10-16 km). It is caused by the sharp temperature difference across the air stream, and blows from west to east in both hemispheres.

K/T boundary K is the traditional abbreviation for the Cretaceous period, and T is the abbreviation for the Tertiary period. The K/T boundary marks the end of the Mesozoic era, and the beginning of the Cenozoic era.

Lithosphere The rigid outermost layer of a planet. On the Earth it lies above the asthenosphere and includes the crust and upper part of the mantle, and is approximately 60 miles (100 km) in depth. The Earth's lithosphere is segmented into plates.

Margin The edge of a tectonic plate, one of the huge slabs of the Earth's lithosphere that support the continents as they slowly drift around.

Maritime climate A maritime climate is the climate typically found along the west coasts at the middle latitudes of all the world's continents, and in southeast Australia.

Metamorphism The process that changes existing rocks minerlogically, but without them entering the liquid phase—that is, without melting.

Monsoon A seasonal wind pattern that brings heavy rain to southern Asia. It blows from the northeast (toward the sea) in winter and rain laden from the southwest (toward the land) in summer. The monsoon cycle is believed to have started about 12 million years ago with the uplift of the Himalayas.

Obliquity The angle that one plane makes with another. For instance, the ecliptic makes an angle of 23° 26' with the celestial equator (because the Earth's equator is inclined at this angle to the orbital plane). This is termed the obliquity of the ecliptic.

Oceanic ridge A global network of ridges crosses the floors of the oceans. They rise many thousands of feet above the abyssal plain, have a linear form, and crests that are dissected by rifting.

Orogenesis The tectonic process that produces fold belts, metamorphism, and magmatism, typically from a sequence of sedimentary rocks that have been involved in plate convergence. The culmination of an orogeny is the uprise of new belts of fold mountains.

Paleontology The study of past life forms through fossil remains. Although fossils have been known and described since pre-Christian times, modern palaeontology developed only during the middle of the 19th century.

Paleopole The last position of the Earth's magnetic poles as determined in rocks from their remnant magnetization.

Pelagic Describes the organisms that inhabit open water and seabirds that spend most of their time far from land. The term is also applied to the upper layers of the ocean where such organisms are found.

Phonolite An extrusive igneous rock intermediate in composition and strongly alkaline. Phonolite contains feldspathoids rather than feldspars and is widespread as lavas in rift valleys.

Plate tectonics The theory of the Earth that invokes the movement of lithospheric plates as an explanation of processes such as volcanism, seismicity, and orogonesis.

Polarity reversal The Earth's magnetic field episodically shows reversals in its polarity, giving rise to magnetic epochs of normal and reversed polarity. Reversals occur at intervals of between 10,000 and 25 million years and give rise to magnetic striping in rocks.

Precession The slow movement of the celestial poles. It is largely due to the wobbling motion of the Earth's rotational axis induced by gravitational attraction of the Moon on Earth's equatorial bulge.

Pyroclast Material that includes large volumes of fine dust, ash, and blocks, ejected from the vent of an exploding volcano. Pyroclasts may enter into gaseous suspension in nuées ardentes, producing pyroclastic flow deposits.

Quartz One of the most widespread silicate minerals of the Earth's continental regions and the chief component in clastic sedimentary rocks. It is mostly silicon dioxide (SiO_2).

Seismometer A sensitive instrument for recording seismic waves. The original instruments used a very sensitive spring to record vibrations caused by seismic events.

Subduction zone The inclined zone at the boundary of two converging lithospheric plates, along which consumption of one plate occurs.

Tectonics The deformation that affects the lithospheres of planets. The term includes folding, thrusting, shearing, and faulting, and any features associated with epeirogenic movements. This may be global or regional in scale.

Temperate Describing a climate typical of mid-latitudes that is intermediate between the extremes of the polar and tropical climates. The temperate zone is considered to be the area between the Arctic Circle and the Topic of Cancer and the Antarctic Circle and the Tropic of Capricorn.

Turbidite A sedimentary rock laid down by a turbidity current. A typical turbidite layer shows graded bedding and sedimentary "bottom structures," which are infills of grooves and hollows eroded into the sea bed by swiftly moving sediment-laden slurries.

Further Research

BOOKS

Aleshire, Peter, and Nash, Geoffrey H. *Ocean Ridges and Trenches* (The Extreme Earth), New York: Chelsea House Publications, 2007.

Aleshire, Peter. *Deserts* (The Extreme Earth), New York: Chelsea House Publications, 2007.

Brezina, Corona. *Climate Change* (In the News), New York: Rosen Publishing Group, 2007.

Bright, Michael. *Changing Ecosystems* (Timeline: Life on Earth), Oxford: Heinemann Educational Books, 2008.

Claybourne, Anna. *Deep Oceans* (Earth's Final Frontiers), Chicago: Heinemann, 2007.

Cooper, Margaret, and Vertut, Jean. *Exploring the Ice Age*, New York: Atheneum, 2001.

DK Publishing. *Ice Age: Dawn of the Dinosaurs Essential Guide* (DK Essential Guides) London: Dorling Kindersley, 2009.

D'Souza, Blanche. *Harnessing the Trade Winds. The Story of the Centuries-Old Indian Trade with East Africa, using the Monsoon Winds*, Kenya: Zand Graphics, 2008.

Edwards, John. *Plate Tectonics And Continental Drift* (Looking at Landscapes), North Mankato, MN: Smart Apple Media, 2005.

Gardner, Robert. *Planet Earth Science Fair Projects: Using The Moon, Stars, Beach Balls, Frisbees, And Other Far-out Stuff*, Berkeley Heights, NJ: Enslow Publishers, 2005.

Holmes, Thom. *Early Life: The Cambrian Period* (The Prehistoric Earth), New York: Chelsea House Publications, 2008.

Kirchner, Renee. *The KidHaven Science Library—Biomes*, Farmington Hills, MI: KidHaven Press, 2006.

Knauer, Kelly. *Time Living Wonders: The Marvels and Mysteries of Life on Earth*, Parsippany, NJ: Time Home Entertainment, 2009.

Lovelock, James. *The Revenge of Gaia: Earth's Climate Crisis & The Fate of Humanity*, New York: Basic Books, 2007.

Miller, Ron. *Earth And The Moon*, Breckenridge, CO: 21st Century, 2003.

INTERNET RESOURCES

The Earth's Moon. A comprehensive guide to the Moon. The site also includes details on recent and future lunar eclipses.
www.windows.ucar.edu/tour/link=/earth/moons_and_rings.html

How Volcanoes Work. This website is a comprehensive educational resource that describes the science behind volcanoes and volcanic processes. Sponsored by NASA, it contains many good illustrations and photographs.
www.geology.sdsu.edu/how_volcanoes_work/

Google Earth—Oceans. This site allows users to examine wildlife, mountains, shipwrecks, and environmental changes in the world's oceans today.
www.guardian.co.uk/environment/2009/feb/02/google-earth-oceans

Ice Ages. A description of the ice ages of the last 2 million years. This site covers many other relevant topics such as climate change, global warming, and continental drift.
www.ace.mmu.ac.uk/eae/Climate_Change/Older/Ice_Ages.html

Paleomap Project. Illustrated with 3D paleogeographic animations, the Paleomap Project shows the plate tectonic development of the ocean basins and continents, as well as the changing distribution of land and sea during the past 1100 million years.
www.scotese.com/Default.htm

Seafloor spreading. Explore the seafloor with the NeMO Explorer. The site covers many related concepts such as mid-ocean ridges, seamounts, hot spots, and hydrothermal vents.
www.pmel.noaa.gov/vents/nemo/explorer/concepts/spreading.htm

River Erosion. Everything you need to know about rivers: their course, speed, volume, ability to change the landscape, and usefulness to people.
library.thinkquest.org/20035/river.htm

Water Science Basics: Glaciers and icecaps. Illustrated with maps and photographs, this is a useful source of information about these enormous stores of freshwater.
ga.water.usgs.gov/edu/earthglacier.html

The World's Biomes. A well-presented site fully covering six major types of biome: freshwater, marine, desert, forest, grassland, and tundra.
www.ucmp.berkeley.edu/exhibits/biomes/index.php

World Climates. The Köppen system of climate classification that is most widely used for classifying the world's climates. The Earth's surface is divided into climatic regions that generally coincide with world patterns of vegetation and soils.
www.blueplanetbiomes.org/climate.htm

Index

Page numbers in **bold** refer to full articles; page numbers in *italic* refer to illustrations and captions.

A

abyssal plains 24, 66, 67
accretion 48
acid rain 82
Agulhas current *94*
air currents 84, 85, 90, 91, 92
Alps *31*, 52
Amazon River 62, 80
Andes mountains *29*, 50, *51*
anorthosite 8
Antarctica 26, 33, *33*, 42, 97
anticyclones 90
aquatic biomes 101
Archean eon 55
Arctic 97
asteroids 6, 9, 10, 55, 56
asthenosphere 12, 14, 20, 36, 43
Atlantic Ocean 46, 47
atmosphere 8, 11, 22-23, 33, 76, 78, 79, 93, 102
atmospheric pressure 83, 84, 85, 90-92
atmospheric processes 8, 23, 33, 68
atolls 66
axial inclination 32
Ayres Rock *42*

B

bacteria 22
barchans 68
basaltic rocks *15*, 24, 45, 59
beaches 66
bedding planes 59
bedforms 68
beneath the ocean floor **45-46**
Benioff zones 49, *51*
biomes 93, **99-101**, *99*
blizzards 87
blue-green algae 77
boreal forest 104
boulder clay 73
Brazil current *94*

C

calder 17
Cambrian period 55, 56, *57*, 77
carbon dioxide 22, 25, 26, 32, 61, 76, 79, 93, 102
chinook 97
cliff erosion 66
climate 40, 83-85, 86-89, 90, 100

climatic zones 83, 84, 85, 99-101
coastal erosion 65, 66
coasts **65-67**
constructive plate margins 45
continental climates 101
continental crusts 27, *29*
continental drift 32, 36, 37, 40-42, *41*, 40, 43, 53
continental growth 28, 29
continental plates 27, *29*, 36, 37
convection currents 93
convective motions 28, 29, 43, 45
convergence zones 24
Cordilleras 51, *51*
cores 7, 12, 13, *13*, 21
Coriolis effect 90, *90*, 91, *94*
craters 10, 11
cratons 27, 40
crevasses *72*
cross-bedding 68
crusts 8, *9*, 10, 11, 36, 37
currents 65
cyclones 90, 91

D

daylength 97, 98, 104
deciduous trees 104
Deep Sea Drilling Project 46
deposition 62, *63*
deserts and winds **68-70**
deserts **68-70**, 85, 99, *100*, 103, 105
destructive plate margins 38
dinosaurs 56, *56*, 77, 82
distributaries *63*
divergent plate margins 39
DNA *76*
Doldrums 91
dreikanter 69
drumlins 72
dune formation *69*
Dynamic planets **8-11**, 18

E

early continents **27-29**
Earth and Moon **6-7**, 8-10, *9*
Earth's atmosphere 10, **22-23**, 78, 79, 83, 93
Earth's crust 10, 14, 15
Earth's oceans **24-26**
Earth's orbit 32, 34, 35, *35*, 96, *96*
Earth's rotation 90, *90*, 91
earthquake focus 20, *21*, 49, 51
earthquakes 18-21, 37, 38, *39*, 49, 50, 51, *67*, 80, 81, 82
East African Rift Valley 53, 54, *54*
East Pacific Rise 23

E (continued)

Easterlies 91, *91*
El Niño 95
Equator 84, *84*, 85, 90, 91, 92
equinoxes *96*
erosion 58, 60, 66, 68, 69, 70, 71
erratics 73
eskers 72
eukaryotes 77
Everest, Mount *35*
evolution 56, 57, *57*, 77
extinction 56, 82

F

faults 53
feldspar 60, *60*, 82
firn *72*
Flandrian 89, *89*
fold mountains 38, 50, 51, *51*, 52, 58
forests 99, 100, *100*, 104
fossil fuels 79
fossils 36, 40, 42, 55, 57, 58
fractional crystallization 14, 15
freeze-thaw activity 68, 74

G

gabbro rocks 24
Gaia Hypothesis **78-79**
gases 22, 23
geological stories **55-57**
geotectonic imagery 45
Giant's Causeway *15*
glacial debris 71-73
glacial geography 71-74
glacial landforms 72-73
glacial maximum 86, 87
glacial striations 71
glaciation 8, 30, 31, 34, 35, 61, 65, 86, 87
glaciers and ice **71-74**, 86, 87, *89*
global climate 32, 35, **83-85**, 86-89, 93, 102, *103*
global conveyor 26, 32, 34
global warming *89*
Gobi Desert 105
Gondwanaland 31, *41*, 42, 53, *57*
graben 53
Grand Canyon 58
granite rocks 27, 59, 60, *60*
granodiorite 47
grasslands 99, *99*, *100*, 103
gravity 6, 59, 93
Great Lakes 87
greenhouse effect 33, 61
Greenland *89*
Gulf Stream 94, *94*

Gutenberg discontinuity 21
Gutenberg, Beno 43

H

hanging valleys 73
Hawaiian Islands 16
helium 75
Herschel, John 32
hibernation 98, 105
Himalayas *31*, 33, *35*, 44, *44*, 52, *52*, 97
Holocene epoch *57*
Homo erectus 77
Homo sapiens 82
horst 53
hot spots 16, 37, *39*, *44*, 48
human ancestors 77
hydrocarbons 75, 76
hydrogen 75, 76
hydrothermal springs 25

I

ice advances 86, 87
ice ages **30-35**, 62, 71, 79, 86-89
ice sheets 71, 86, 87, 88
ice **71-74**, 86-89
icebergs *31*
Iceland *46*
igneous rocks 12, 28, 38
infrared radiation 22,
inner core 12
interglacials 30, 72, 86, *89*
iridium 82
island arcs 28, **47-49**, 48, *48*, 49, 50
island chains 44, *44*
isostacy 75
isotopes 8,

J

jet streams *91*, 92
Jupiter 6, *23*

K

K/T boundary 82
Kenya *83*
Kilimanjaro 54
Kuroshio current *94*

L

lahars 16
Laurasia 31, 41, 42, *57*
lava *11*, 12, *17*
life on Earth **75-77**

limestone 61
lithosphere 10, 11, 36, 43, 44, 45, *48*, 50
Lovelock, James 78, 79
lunar eclipses 7

M

magma and volcanoes **12-17**
magma 9, 10, 11, 12-17, 39, 43, 50
magmatism 38, 48
magnetic poles 41, 42
magnetic striping 46
mammal evolution 56, *56*, 77, 82
mantle 8, 12-14, 21, 24, 27, 28, 36, 43
Mariana trench 47, *49*
maritime climates 101
Mars 6, 8, 11, 18, 32, 55, 56
meanders *63*
Mediterranean Sea 47
meltwater *73*
Mercury 6, 8, 11, 55
mesosphere 12
Mesozoic era 26, 31
metabolism 78
metamorphism 27, 38, 48, 50
meteorites 6, 9, 10, 21, 28, 55, 76, 82
Mid-Atlantic Ridge *25*, 46, *46*
migration 97, *98*, 105
Milankovitch cycle 34, *34*
Milankovitch, Milutin 32, 34
Milford Sound *71*
minerals 58, 59, 60, *60*, 61, 79
Mississippi River 62
mistral 97
mobile and stable zones **36-39**, *39*
Mohorovicic discontinuity 21
monoliths *59*
monsoon 97
Moon 6, 7, *7*, 10, 11, 18, 55
moons 6
moraine *72*, 73
moraine deposits 30
mountain avens 89
mountain-building 27, 33, *37*, 38, 44, 50, 55, 58
mountains from the sea **50-52**
moving oceans **93-95**

N

natural catastrophes **80-82**
Nazca plate 50, *51*
Neptune 6
nuclear winters 35
nuées ardentes 16

O

obliquity 35
ocean currents 26, 88, 94, *94*, 95
ocean ridges 15, 24, 25, *25*, 39, 43, 45, 46, 51
oceanic basalt 16
oceanic circulation 26
oceanic plates 27, 28, 29, 38, 43
oceanic trenches 24, *25*, 47, *49*
oceans 23, 24-26, *39*, 47, **65-67**, **93-95**
orbits 6, 7
Ordovician period *57*
organic oozes 67
orogenesis 10, 38, 50, 51, *51*, 58
outer core 12, 21
oxygen 76, 77, 78
ozone 23, 76

P

P waves 19, *19*, 20, *21*
Pacific Ocean *39*, 47
Pacific Rim *39*, 47
pahoehoe *11*
paleolatitude 40
paleomagnetism 40, 42, 46
paleontology 36, 58
paleopoles 41
Paleozoic era 31, 41
Pangea 26, *30*, 31, *41*, 42, *57*
partial melting 14
permafrost 74, 105, *105*
Peru current 95
Phanerozoic eon 56
phase changes 13
phonolite 54
photoionization 23
photosynthesis 22, 77
Pinatubo, Mount 16, 80
pingos 74
plagioclase feldspar 8
planetary atmospheres *23*
planets 6-11, *23*, 59, 75
plankton 95
plate margins 15, 24, 37, 47, 51, 66
plate tectonics 10, 24, 28, 32, 36, 37, 43, 78
plateaus 70
plates and plumes **43-44**
playa 70
Pleistocene epoch 30, *57*, 62, *73*
Pliocene epoch 56
polar biomes 100, *100*, 103
polar ice-caps 33
polar regions 84, 85, *100*, 101
poles 30, 31, 41, 46, 68, 84, 85, 90, 91

power sources 79
prairies 104
Precambrian era 55, *57*
precession 31, 32, 35
primordial crusts 27
prokaryotes 77
pyroclasts 16, 17, *17*

R

rainfall 62, 70, 85, 90, 99, 102
rainforests 85, 102, *102*, *103*
Rayleigh Taylor instabilities 14
regolith 10
retreating ice *73*
reversed polarity 46
Richter Scale 18, *18*, 19, 81
rift faults 54
rift valleys **53-54**, *54*
Ring of Fire 47
river channels *63*
river debris 63, 65
river deltas 62, *63*, 65
river load 62, 64
rivers **62-64**, *64*, 65, 88
roches moutonées 71
rock arches *59*, 70
rotational axis 35

S

S waves 19, *19*, 20, *21*
Sahara desert 68, *69*
Saharan shield 40
salinity 24, 25, 26
saltwater biomes *100*
San Andreas Fault 51, 81
sand dunes 68, 69, *69*
Saturn 6
savanna grasslands *83*, *99*, *103*, 104
sea ice 97
sea levels 88
sea-floor spreading 28, 29, 37, *44*, 45, 46
seasonal changes **96-98**
seasonal winds 97
seawater density 26
sedimentary rocks 27, 50, 58, 59
sedimentation 38, 61, 65
seif dunes *69*
seismic discontinuities 21, *29*

seismic waves **18-21**, 20, 21, 81
seismicity 10, 13, 18, 38, *39*, 47, 66, *67*
seismographs 18, 19
seismometer 18, 20
shadow zones 20, *20*, 21, *21*
silicates 12, 14, 22, 58
Silurian period *57*
solar heating 23, 34
solar radiation 76, 78
Solar System 6, 8, 55, 75, 78
solstices *96*
South Equatorial current 95
spreading axes 43
St. Helens, Mount 16, 80
star dunes *69*
steppes 104
stishovite 82
stratigraphy 36, **58-61**
stratovolcanoes 54
subduction zones *37*, *39*, 44, *48*, 49, *49*, *51*, 52
subsidence 53
Sun 6, 7, 8, 22, 26, 31, 56, 75, 83, 96, *96*
supercontinent 40, *41*, 42, 53

T

taiga 104
tail dunes *69*
technology 79
tectonic plates 15, 16, 18, 24
tectonic processes 8, 14, 18, 27
temperate biomes 100, 101, *103*, 104
temperate forests 104
temperate regions 84, 85, 91, 92, 96, 99, 100, *100*, *103*
terminal moraine 71, *72*
terrestrial biomes 100, *100*, 102, *103*
terrestrial magmas 12
Tethys Sea *41*, 42
thermosphere 23
tides 6, 66
tillites 30, 74
timber 104
trace elements 13
trade winds *84*, 91, *91*, 92
transform faults 51
tributaries 62

tropical biomes *100*, 102, *103*
tropical rainforests 102, *102*
tropical regions 84, 85, 96, 97, 99, 100, *100*
tropopause 23
troposphere 22, 23, 68
tundra *74*, *103*, 104, 105, *105*
turbidites 66, 67
turbidity currents 67, *67*

U

ultraviolet radiation 23, 76
Uluru *42*
underwater mountains *25*, *37*
Universe 56
upper mantle 12
Uranus 6, *23*
U-shaped valleys 71, *71*

V

Venus 6, 8, 11, 55, 56, 61
Victoria Falls *64*
volcanic activity 8, 9, 10, 11, 37, *44*, *46*, 47, 50, 51, 53
volcanic ash 80, *81*
volcanoes 10, 11, *11*, 12, 15, 18, 28, 32, 38, *39*, 44, *48*, 80, *81*

W

wadis 70
wandering continents **40-42**
water cycle 93
wave action 65, 66
weather forecasts 92
weather patterns **90-92**, 96
weather systems 23, 79, 92
weathering 59, 60, 71, 82
Wegner, Alfred 36, 40
Westerlies 91, *91*
whales *95*
white storks 98
winds 8, 23, **68-70**, 87, 95, 97
world biomes **99-101**

Z

Zambezi River *64*

CC

DATE DUE

Central Childrens

Thomas Crane Public Library